Natural Healing and *Rodale* present

Household Herbs

TIPS ON COOKING AND CLEANING WITH HERBS

Tina James and Louise Gruenberg

RODALE

This book is a compilation of *Cooking with Herbs* (© 1999 Storey Communications, Inc.) and *Herbal Home Hints* (© 1999 Louise Gruenberg), previously published by Rodale Inc. by arrangement with Storey Communications, Inc.

Text and text illustrations © 2002 by Storey Communications, Inc.

Chapters 1, 2, and 5 were written by Tina James. Chapters 3 and 4 were written by Louise Gruenberg.

All rights reserved. No part of this publication may be reproduced or transmitted in any form or by any means, electronic or mechanical, including photocopy, recording, or any other information storage and retrieval system, without the written permission of the publisher.

The information in this book has been carefully researched, and all efforts have been made to ensure accuracy. Rodale Inc. assumes no responsibility for any injuries suffered or for damages or losses incurred during the use of or as a result of following this information. It is important to study all directions carefully before taking any action based on the information and advice presented in this book. When using any commercial product, *always* read and follow label directions. Where trade names are used, no discrimination is intended and no endorsement by Rodale Inc. is implied.

Text Designer: Eugenie Seidenberg Delaney
Cover Designer: Marjorie Vree
All illustrations by Beverly K. Duncan with the exception of those by Brigita Fuhrmann, pages 22, 28, 35, and 49; Sarah Brill, page 24; Charles Joslin, pages 32, 38, 41, 58, and 60; and Mallory Lake, page 73.

Printed in the United States

ISBN 1–57954–717–6

2 4 6 8 10 9 7 5 3 1 paperback

Contents

INTRODUCTION V

CHAPTER 1: YOUR ESSENTIAL HERBAL PANTRY 1
Exploring the Possibilities of Herbal Cooking 2
Using Herbs in Your Cooking 5
Equipping Your Kitchen for Herb Cookery 8
Combining Herbal Flavors 8
Herb Butters 11
Herb Teas 13
Herb Jellies 16
Herb Honeys 18

CHAPTER 2: DELICIOUS SEASONAL HERBAL RECIPES 19
Spring Recipes 20
Summer Recipes 30
Autumn Recipes 41
Winter Recipes 53

CHAPTER 3: BEGINNER'S GUIDE TO HERBAL HOUSEKEEPING 63
Benefits of Herbal Housekeeping 64
Essential Supplies 67
Basic Ingredients 71
Simple Techniques for Herbal Solutions 74

CHAPTER 4: HERBAL HOUSEKEEPING RECIPES 85
Scouring Powders 86
Surface Cleaners 89
Glass Cleaners 91
Metal Polishes 93

Carpet and Rug Cleaners 95
Furniture and Woodwork Cleaners and Polishes 97
Laundry Aids 101
Leather Cleaners 110
Air Fresheners and Sweeteners 112
Your Herbal Cleaning Closet 119
Herbal Housekeeping Ingredients 120
Essential Oils for Housekeeping 124
Fixatives for Housekeeping 126

CHAPTER 5: GROWING, PRESERVING, AND USING HERBS 131

Where to Grow Herbs 132
Laying the Groundwork 133
Digging In 138
Seeds and Transplants 138
Growing-Season Care 140
The Potted Herb 141
All in Good Thyme: An Herb Garden Calendar 143
Herbs Anythyme: The Indoor Herb Garden 145
Harvesting and Storing Herbs 146
Drying Herbs for Winter Use 148
Freezing Herbs for Fresh Flavor 150

Herbal Resources 152

Introduction

We have a special relationship with herbs. It's almost a love affair of sorts. When we catch the aroma of sweet basil or oregano, fantasies of Italian cuisine form in our head. When we taste savory garlic, our taste buds sing. And when we enjoy the soothing beauty and scent of lavender flowers, sweet dreams seem only a pillow away. Herbs connect us to the pleasures of nature through their colors, textures, scents, and tastes.

But the passion we feel for herbs doesn't deny their practicality. Herbs are useful, as you'll discover in the chapters that follow. Whether in your pantry or your cleaning closet, these natural beauties have a lot to offer.

So let our tour guides, authors Tina James and Louise Gruenberg, take you on a journey, sharing much of what they've learned about growing and using herbs.

In Chapter 1, Your Essential Herbal Pantry, you'll find many suggestions for incorporating herbs into your daily cooking, as well as some basic recipes for herb blends, butters, teas, honeys, and jellies. Then get ready to get cooking in Chapter 2, as you discover delicious herbal recipes season by season.

Ever dreamed of beautifying your home and cleaning in a way that supports your family's health? In Chapter 3, Beginner's Guide to Herbal Housekeeping, you'll begin your herbal housekeeping education by learning about the supplies and equipment you'll need, along with simple, basic methods for formulating home care products.

In Chapter 4, Herbal Housekeeping Recipes, you'll find dozens of formulas developed to clean and care for everything from glass and metal to carpets and leather. This chapter also contains some quick, easy, and fun projects for sachets, air fresheners, and simmering potpourris. Reference charts describe herbal housekeeping ingredients, their uses, and where to find them.

Chapter 5 provides everything you need to get started growing, preserving, and using herbs. Several herb garden designs will help you integrate a beautiful and useful garden into your own yard, porch, patio, or deck.

And don't forget to check out Herbal Resources for trustworthy sources of the supplies you'll need—from seeds to storage bottles. On every page of this book, you'll discover tips for enjoying your garden and harvest, whether you have a large herb garden, a few herbs tucked into flower or vegetable beds, or pots of herbs growing on your deck or balcony. Here's to herbs!

CHAPTER 1

YOUR ESSENTIAL
Herbal Pantry

Chocolate pudding was my first signature dish and my dear daddy was kind enough to savor it. Buoyed by early acclaim, I've licked many pots and now stir without standing on a stool. My rules for cooking have been distilled over the years to a simple maxim that translates to living as well. I want the food I serve to be beautiful and nourishing: that is, to delight the eye, smell divine, taste scrumptious, and satisfy completely. Using herbs artfully with garden-fresh ingredients is the best way I know to prepare delightful food. Just breathing in the fragrance of basil and rosemary inspires homage to the simple pleasures that bring joy to each day. And, as a little girl discovered long ago, something good to eat and a few kind words carry us a long way down the road.

Exploring the Possibilities of Herbal Cooking

Nothing compares to the aroma of chopping spicy-fresh marjoram or mincing a bunch of pungent dill. Think about zesting a lemon and the burst of essential oil that you can taste without its entering your mouth. Fresh herbs give food that same lively zip without overpowering the taste buds. In addition to fresh herb leaves and blossoms, some recipes in this book call for herb seeds like cumin, and spices like cinnamon and cloves. In this chapter, you'll find many suggestions for incorporating herbs into your daily cooking, as well as some basic recipes for herb blends, butters, teas, honeys, and jellies.

MATCHING HERBS TO FOODS

Certain herbs seem to have a love affair with particular foods. Who can argue that tomatoes and basil are a perfect match? If you're new to cooking with herbs, take time to identify the flavor of individual herbs. Crush a leaf of savory between your fingers and enjoy the scent. What comes to mind? If your background is German, where savory and green beans go hand in hand, your immediate association may very well be green beans! Nibble on a cinnamon basil leaf. What does it taste like? Close your eyes and try to imagine what foods each of these herb flavors will enhance. Now begin to experiment in the kitchen. Mince a few leaves and use them in dishes where their flavor will stand out, such as a simple salad or an omelet, a cup of tea, or buttered toast. You'll soon be able to create from a whole repertoire of fresh flavor combinations.

The Herb-Food Partnerships chart on page 4 suggests some herb-food marriages made in heaven. After experimenting with these combinations and finding some favorites, take a creative leap and explore inspirations that come to you.

The tomato-basil flavor "marriage" seems to have been made in heaven.

Household Herbs

THE ALLURE OF FRESH HERBS

Fresh herbs, such as parsley, chives, cilantro, basil, and dill, are much preferred over dried herbs for garnishing dishes like salads, omelets, salsas, and vegetables. I'm able to grow most of my own culinary herbs and can harvest something fresh in all but the coldest months in my Zone 6b growing area. To prolong the supply, I bring the rosemary and bay indoors. I also mulch the thyme, chives, Italian parsley, and mint with shredded oak leaves. With a little luck, I can usually find fresh pickings until Christmas.

> **Lively Spices**
>
> For freshest flavor, buy whole seeds and spices and grind them in a coffee grinder before adding them to a recipe.

Fortunately, it's easy to grow fresh basil, cilantro, Italian parsley, dill, and watercress, all of which make excellent — and super nutritious — pesto. If you don't garden, many markets now stock these herbs.

But even if you love to garden, you probably can't grow all of the herbs and spices you'll need for cooking throughout the year. Some herbs need a long, warm growing season (cumin and sesame seed, for example) and are difficult to grow in most parts of North America. If garden space is limited, grow the herbs you enjoy using fresh, especially those that you need in such large quantity that they would be expensive to buy. Organically grown Italian parsley, dill, and cilantro are now available at many groceries for a modest price. Purchase those herbs, and use the saved garden space for basil or marjoram, which may be more costly or harder to find fresh. Or, devote extra space to mint or tarragon, which are needed in abundance for vinegar making.

Large quantities of herbs like fresh basil and parsley are essential for pesto making.

Herb-Food Partnerships

HERB	CHARACTERISTICS	COMPLEMENTARY FOODS
Basil	Clovelike flavor with a hint of mint	Tomatoes, corn, zucchini, green salads, cheese and other dairy dishes, chicken, fish
Bay	Spicy evergreen flavor	Soups and stews, poached fish, pasta sauce; add a bay leaf to the water when cooking noodles or other pasta
Chervil	Delicate parsley flavor with a hint of anise	Eggs, fish, shellfish, asparagus, peas, potatoes, beets
Chives	Mild onion flavor	Cold soups; dairy-based dips, spreads, and dressings; vegetables; eggs
Garlic chives	Mild garlic flavor	Garlic substitute, stir-fries, salads
Cilantro	Earthy, sagey, citrusy (detractors claim it tastes "soapy")	Spicy (Indian, Mexican, and Thai) cuisines, in dishes such as salsa, curry, chili; counters highly seasoned foods
Dill	Sweet and tangy	Hot and cold fish, yogurts, soups, dips, beans, cabbage, pickles, and cold salads like shrimp, potato, and cucumber
Marjoram	Sweet oregano-like flavor	Chicken, most summer vegetables (peas, summer squash, beans, corn, and tomatoes)
Mint	Sweet and pungent	Yogurt dishes, peas, carrots, fruit salads; traditionally associated with lamb
Oregano	Assertive peppery flavor	Highly seasoned dishes, tomato-based preparations; associated with Greek and Italian cuisines
Parsley	Fresh flavor	Almost any dish that isn't sweet; very nutritious; Italian flat-leaved parsley more flavorful; curly parsley for garnishing
Sage	Smoky flavor, somewhat bitter	Poultry stuffing, succotash; associated with wild game
Savory	Peppery	Beans, summer squash, vegetable soups
Tarragon	Distinctive anise flavor	French cuisine (vinaigrette dressing and béarnaise sauce), chicken, fish, meats, potatoes, asparagus, beets, spinach
Thyme	Fresh lemony flavor with a spicy aftertaste	French cuisine, eggs, cheese, poultry, fish, meats, soups, cream sauces, onions, peas, mushrooms

WHEN YOU DON'T HAVE FRESH HERBS

Although nothing compares to the aroma of chopping fresh basil, dried or frozen herbs stand in nicely for fresh herbs during the winter months. Preserving your own herbs is easy (see page 148) and gives one the primal satisfaction of stocking up for the cold months ahead. You can also buy good quality dried herbs. I've found the highest quality herbs from health-food stores, gourmet produce shops, and mail-order suppliers. (See page 152.)

The cost is very reasonable if you buy in bulk rather than pay for fancy packaging. The criteria for selection is simple: The herbs should smell fresh and, if they're from green plants, they should be bright green in color.

Using Herbs in Your Cooking

Ready to make a green salad with fresh herbs? Let's use garlic chives, marjoram, and parsley. Shake the herbs into the sink. If you see any dirt, rinse the herbs quickly under cool water and shake. Spin the herbs in a salad spinner to dry — or wrap them loosely in a towel or pillowcase and go outside and shake them hard.

MINCING METHODS

Scissors work well for mincing in most instances. To mince the blades of herbs like garlic chives, hold a small bunch of them over the salad or a bowl and snip into tiny pieces using sharp kitchen scissors. For soft-stalked herbs like parsley, dill, and cilantro, you needn't strip the leaves; simply trim away tough stems, roll the leaves into a small ball, and then take tiny snips, cutting right through the ball.

For woody-stemmed herbs like marjoram, thyme, sage, and rosemary, strip the leaves from the stems (unless the stems are very tender, in which case you can treat them as you do parsley), cut the herbs coarsely with scissors into a teacup, then cut them against the sides of the cup until the greens are finely minced. I like to sprinkle minced herbs directly on the salad, but you can also add them to a salad dressing.

For a large quantity of herbs, it may be easier and faster to use a sharp chef's knife and cutting board than scissors. Remove the stems or strip the leaves as described above, and lay the leaves flat on the board. Use one hand to position the leaves and the other to chop. In most cases, it's best to "mince fine," that is, chop until the herbs are cut into tiny bits. Coarse chopping will do if the herbs are to be pureed, as in pesto.

Some people use a food processor to mince fresh herbs. Unless you're very careful, however, machines can turn tender herbs into mush. And then you have to clean the machine! It's just not worth it for small amounts. I do use a standard-size food processor for pesto, however, and a coffee grinder to grind dry herbs.

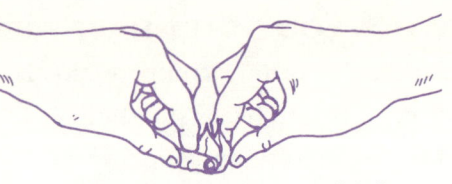

Roll several leaves into a small ball, then snip with scissors or a knife.

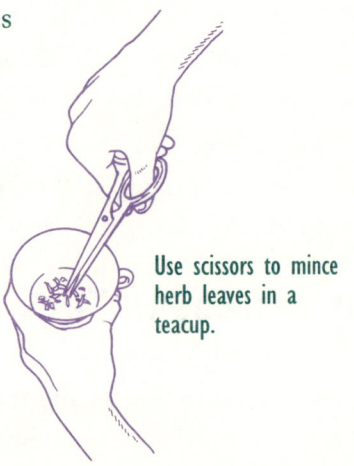

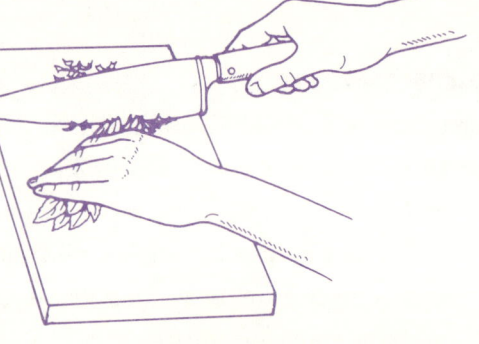

Use scissors to mince herb leaves in a teacup.

Mince large bundles of herbs on a cutting board.

WHEN TO ADD FRESH HERBS

Mix fresh herbs into salad dressings and sauces and use them to garnish the final presentation as well. In cooked dishes, add the

> ### How to Measure Herbs
>
> - Mound dried herbs on the measuring spoon. Then use your fingers to crumble them into foods.
> - Measure ground herbs by the level spoonful.
> - Pack minced fresh herbs to measure.
> - Use two to three times more fresh herbs when substituting them for dried herbs in a recipe. Use the lower end of the range for strongly flavored herbs like rosemary and sage.
> - To substitute dried herbs for fresh, crush a few leaves in your hands. If they smell very fresh, use one-third as much. If the aroma is faint, use half as much. Fresh herbs are unlikely to overpower a dish, but it's better to err on the side of caution with dried herbs.

woodier fresh herbs (sage, thyme, rosemary, tarragon) during the last half hour of cooking. If you're using delicate herbs like cilantro, basil, dill, chives, marjoram, or parsley, stir them into the dish a minute or two before serving. When I make soups, I often put freshly minced herbs in the bottom of each soup bowl and then ladle the soup over the herbs. The hot liquid infuses the herb and captures its fresh flavor.

WHEN TO ADD DRIED HERBS

Ground herbs have a more intense flavor and dissolve into the food, so diners won't notice the texture of the dried leaves. If you have whole or crumbled dried herbs, rub them between your fingers or zip them (singly or in a blend; see page 8) in a coffee grinder until they are finely ground. Once ground, the flavorful essential oils dissipate rapidly, so prepare ground herbs in small batches and use them within a month.

For salad dressings and sauces, add the dried herbs and let stand at least 10 minutes in order to rehydrate the herb and to allow flavors to mingle. For cooked dishes like soups and stews, add woody herbs when assembling the ingredients. Crumble the herbs with your fingers. If you're using more delicate herbs, add them 10 to 15 minutes before serving, again crumbling the leaves with your fingers.

EQUIPPING YOUR KITCHEN FOR HERB COOKERY

The bare-bones list of supplies includes a pair of sharp scissors that feel comfortable in your hand for mincing herbs, a chef's knife for chopping herbs and garlic, and a mortar and pestle for grinding seeds and herb blends. Although for centuries cooks made pesto using only a mortar and pestle, a food processor is much faster. Faster isn't always better, though — the noise certainly isn't soothing — but I confess to using the modern method here. I also rely on a coffee grinder to grind large amounts of seeds and dried herbs. By the way, don't try to use the same gadget for grinding coffee and herbs. Both leave indelible flavors that resist even the most ardent attempts at cleaning. To clean, wipe the reservoir with a paper towel after each use. A small food processor is another option, but it doesn't grind as uniformly as a coffee grinder.

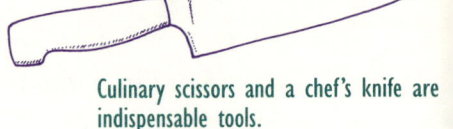

Culinary scissors and a chef's knife are indispensable tools.

COMBINING HERBAL FLAVORS

Although any herb tastes great alone, blended herbs develop richer flavors. Begin your experimenting by composing a tried-and-true herb blend as a springboard. The classic French mixture called *fines herbes* consists of chives (onion family), chervil (carrot family), thyme (mint family), and often tarragon. Each "family" of herbs shares similar flavor characteristics. (See Flavor Families on page 9.) You can play with the basic fines herbes formula, combining one or more herbs from each family to produce dozens of variations.

A few oddballs seem to refuse to fit neatly in any category. Although anise-flavored tarragon, in the composite family, combines

Household Herbs

> **Flavor Families**
>
> **Onion family.** Chives, garlic chives, garlic, leek, bulb onions, scallions (or green onions), shallots
> **Carrot family.** Anise, caraway, celery, chervil, cilantro/coriander, cumin, dill, fennel, lovage, parsley. Use seeds or leaves for different flavors.
> **Mint family.** Basil, lemon balm, marjoram, mints, oregano, rosemary, sage, savory, thyme

with the onion family and neutral herbs like parsley and thyme, it's best on its own. Bay leaves, in the laurel family, have a mildly spicy evergreen flavor, good in soups and stews; bay blends with many herbs.

BOUQUET GARNI

A *bouquet garni* is a small bunch of fresh herbs gathered together with string (or tied up in a piece of muslin or an unbleached coffee filter) and dropped into soups and stews during the last half hour of cooking. A *bouquet garni* needs no chopping and is easy to fish out of the pot after cooking. Although a bouquet garni is usually used for cooking, a fresh one is also pretty inserted into napkin rings!

Tuck a bunch of fresh herbs into a napkin ring.

A standard bouquet consists of a bay leaf, a few sprigs of thyme, two or three parsley stalks, and often a sprig of tarragon. Vary the combination of herbs in your bouquet according to the foods in the dish. Here are some delicious blends to start with:

With vegetables: parsley, savory, thyme, and bay
With chicken: marjoram, rosemary, and savory; fennel, rosemary, and bay; parsley, bay, and lemongrass
With turkey: sage, bay, and parsley
With fish: tarragon and parsley; fennel, bay, and lemon thyme; dill, parsley, and mint

Your Essential Herbal Pantry

A FEW ALL-PURPOSE HERB BLENDS

I don't make many dried herb blends because I prefer to smell and taste while adding each ingredient. The following combinations are so versatile, however, that it's worth preparing a month's supply. They're also handy for doctoring prepared foods.

The instructions for each mix are the same: Simply combine all ingredients and then store in airtight containers. Crumble or grind the herbs when adding them to foods. Mixes are best used within 3 to 6 months.

Poultry Seasoning

The herbs in this traditional mixture are tried-and-true seasonings for roasting chicken and livening up stuffing. I use them in Uncle Bicky's Not-Red Barbecued Chicken (page 29). Poultry Seasoning also enlivens steamed vegetables, rice, and stir-fries. Makes ½ cup.

- 3 tablespoons lemon thyme
- 2 tablespoons marjoram
- 1 tablespoon sage
- 1 tablespoon rosemary
- 2 teaspoons freshly ground black pepper
- ½ teaspoon nutmeg

Italian Seasoning

Mediterranean herbs are a great way to entice "just meat-and-potato eaters" down the herbal path. Use this savory blend to perk up tomato sauce, pizza sauce, roasted vegetables, and salad dressing. Makes about ½ cup.

- 3 tablespoons basil
- 2 tablespoons oregano or marjoram
- 1 tablespoon thyme
- 2 teaspoons rosemary

Sweet Potato Unfries

Here's a tasty and nutritious snack with very little fat. Preheat the oven to 425°F. Spray a baking sheet with nonstick cooking spray. Scrub some sweet potatoes but do not peel them. Cut the potatoes into ⅛-inch slices. Place them in a single layer on the baking sheet, and brush them lightly with olive oil. Sprinkle generously with Cajun Blend (recipe below). Bake for 15 minutes. Turn the slices and bake 5 minutes more. Enjoy this spicy treat hot.

Cajun Blend

The sweet and spicy zest of this Cajun mixture is ideal for seasoning fish and chicken before grilling. It's also good on popcorn. Makes about 1¼ cups.

- 5 tablespoons paprika
- 5 tablespoons thyme
- 2 tablespoons oregano or marjoram
- 2 tablespoons freshly ground black pepper
- 2 tablespoons garlic powder
- 1 tablespoon kosher salt (optional)
- 1 tablespoon cayenne pepper
- 1 teaspoon cumin seed
- 1 teaspoon ground ginger
- ½ teaspoon ground cloves

HERB BUTTERS

Combining fresh herbs and unsalted butter creates a versatile seasoning for cooked vegetables, hot breads, soups and chowders, and baked fish. Plus, it really perks up canned soups and frozen vegetables. Herb butters also freeze well, so this is an excellent way to preserve garden-fresh flavors — particularly chervil and dill, which don't dry well.

As a general rule, use 5 tablespoons of minced fresh herbs to 1 stick of softened unsalted (sweet) butter. Blend well and refrigerate in an airtight container for up to ten days, or freeze for longer storage. Use your favorite individual herbs or combine flavors. See Herb-Butter Partnerships, below, for some favorite combinations to get you started.

If you're trying to lower cholesterol, make Better Butter. Combine ½ cup cold-pressed vegetable oil with ½ cup softened, unsalted butter. Then use the Herb-Butter combinations below. Better Butter freezes well, too. (Cold-pressed vegetable oil is extracted by methods that don't involve heat, thereby preserving important nutrients like vitamin E. Use this oil in recipes that you don't cook, such as herb butters or salad dressings. It's available in health-food stores and gourmet shops.)

Herb-Butter Partnerships

HERBS	USES
Equal parts parsley, chervil, and chives	All-purpose
Equal parts dill, chervil, and chives	All-purpose
Equal parts burnet or borage, chervil, and chives	All-purpose
Equal parts lemon balm, chives, and parsley	Fish, vegetables
Equal parts chervil, chives, and mint	Fish, carrots, peas
Equal parts marjoram and basil	Chicken, peas, carrots, corn, squash
Equal parts calendula petals, chives, and parsley	Pretty on vegetables and rice
2 parts nasturtium flowers, to 1 part nasturtium leaves, to ½ teaspoon of lemon juice	Hot breads; great cucumber sandwich spread!
Scented geranium flowers, rose petals, or dianthus blossoms	Scones, waffles, muffins
Calamint (*Calamintha nepeta*) blossoms with a squeeze of lemon juice (calamint blossoms have a delightful peppery-mint flavor)	Delicious on peas, mushrooms, carrots, biscuits
Mixed herb and flower blossoms (such as thyme, chicory, borage, calendula, 'Lemon Gem' marigold, opal basil, lavender, carnation, clove pinks)	Beautiful for biscuits, scones

Herb Teas

Herb teas are a pleasant "decaf" beverage and offer endless variety. The eleven all-purpose blends below work well for both fresh and dried herbs. Feel free to add herbs to black or decaf tea. Then be sure to see A Perfect Pot of Herb Tea (on page 14) for brewing directions.

- 4 parts rosemary and 1 part lavender (good hot or iced with Earl Grey tea!)
- 2 parts lemon balm and 1 part sage
- 2 parts peppermint and 1 part yarrow
- 1 part lemon verbena and 1 part bergamot flowers
- 1 part mint and 1 part alfalfa
- 4 parts spearmint, 2 parts chamomile, and 1 part rosemary
- 1 part thyme, 1 part bergamot flowers, and a pinch of ground ginger
- 2 parts linden flowers, 1 part rosemary, and 1 part gingerroot
- 1 part peppermint, 1 part basil, and 1 part thyme
- 2 parts marjoram, 1 part mint, and a little orange peel
- 8 parts spearmint, 4 parts peppermint, 4 parts anise hyssop, 1 part sage, and 1 part rosemary

Super Sweet Stevia

Stevia (*Stevia rebaudiana*) is the most powerful sweetener yet discovered, 10 to 15 times sweeter by volume than sugar. Two or three leaves will sweeten 4 to 6 cups of tea, and has little effect on other herb flavors. This Zone 9 herb is easy to grow in a pot and to propagate by seed or cuttings. It can also be grown as an annual; the leaves are easy to dry. The best news is that stevia contains virtually no calories, does not adversely affect blood sugar levels, and causes no known ill effects. South American cultures have used the herb for centuries. (For plant and seed sources, see page 152.)

Stevia

Your Essential Herbal Pantry

A Perfect Pot of Herb Tea

Here's how to make a perfect pot of tea. It takes only a few extra minutes to enjoy much more flavor, and the whole process, like the tea itself, is satisfying and relaxing. You'll need two china or glass teapots, one for brewing, the other for serving, and a bamboo or wire-mesh strainer.

> Freshly boiled water (spring or distilled water is best)
> 1 heaping tablespoon fresh herbs *or* 1 mounded teaspoon dried herbs per cup of boiling water
> Lemon and honey (optional)

1. Heat the water and pour a little into both teapots to warm them.
2. Empty the water from the brewing pot, measure the herbs into it, and then pour boiling water over them. Cover the pot and let tea steep for 5 minutes.
3. Empty the hot water out of the serving pot. Pour the tea through a strainer into the serving pot or directly into warmed teacups. Serve with the optional lemon and honey.

Easy Homemade Tea Filter

Crumbling herbs into tea bags dissipates essential oils and greatly shortens storage life. Brewing tea with "loose" dried herbs doesn't have to be complicated, however, when you use this easy-to-make tea "filter" fashioned from an unbleached round coffee filter. To make, fold the filter in half. Then fold it in thirds toward the middle to form a cone. When you open the cone, you have a leakproof filter. Pierce two holes in the edge of the cone as shown, and insert a dried herb stalk or skewer through the holes to support the filter in the cup. Voilà! Tea filters can be reused several times before composting.

Tonic Teas

Herb teas can be more than a refreshing beverage. Some varieties can help you treat specific health problems. Consult a book on herbal remedies for advice on which herbs are most effective for which conditions. In addition, you can brew tonic teas, which are simply strong infusions of food-quality herbs brewed for a longer period than regular tea so as to extract all the nutrients. They are designed to be an integral part of a health maintenance program. To keep you feeling healthy, try this tonic tea recipe. Prepare a large jarful of this mixture and use it immediately, or store it, covered tightly, in a cool, dark place for up to 6 months. Or, make the blend with fresh herbs for immediate use.

> 2 parts dried peppermint — rich in calcium
> 1 part dried oatstraw *(Avena sativa)* — nerve strengthener
> 1 part dried nettle *(Urtica dioica)* — rich in iron, chlorophyll, and amino acids
> 1 part dried chickweed *(Stellaria media)* — rich in minerals, especially silica
> 1 part dried red clover heads *(Trifolium pratense)* — good blood cleanser
> 1 part dried alfalfa leaf — rich in iron, vitamins, and minerals
> ½ part dried lemon balm — calming and calcium-rich
> ¼ part dried chamomile — good digestive

1. Place 2 heaping tablespoons of the dried herb mixture (6 to 8 tablespoons of fresh herbs) in a 2-quart, heatproof container. Fill with boiling water.
2. Cover the container with a folded tea towel. To gather all the goodness, let sit at least 2 hours before drinking. (I let mine sit overnight.) Refrigerate if not consumed within 8 hours. You can flavor the tea with lemon, honey, or both if you wish.

Herb Jellies

Herb jelly is a delicate delight to spread on any hot bread. You can also use it in glazes or marinades. Because the basic recipe calls for infusing the jelly with fresh herbs twice, the result is extra flavorful. See page 17 for suggestions for herb and liquid combinations. The basic recipe makes 6 cups.

BASIC METHOD FOR MAKING HERB JELLY

   2 cups boiling water
   2 cups packed fresh herb leaves
   2½ cups (approximately) unsweetened apple juice
   3½ cups granulated sugar
   1 package Sure-Gel or other low-sugar pectin
   2 cups fresh herb sprigs
   4 tablespoons cider vinegar
   1 herb sprig for each jar, for garnish

1. Wash six half-pint or three one-pint canning jars and jar rings in the dishwasher or in hot soapy water. Rinse well. Place jars, rings, and new vacuum lids in gently boiling water until you are ready for them.
2. Pour the boiling water over the fresh herb leaves; infuse for 1 hour. Strain. Measure the infusion into a large saucepan. Add enough apple juice to make 4½ cups total liquid.
3. In a small bowl, mix ¼ cup of the sugar with the pectin. Whisk into herb infusion, and bring to a rolling boil. Stir in remaining sugar; return to a boil. Boil hard for 1 full minute. Remove from the heat. Stir in 2 cups fresh herb sprigs. Cover; let steep for 5 minutes.
4. With tongs, pull out the herbs. Skim off the foam. Stir in the vinegar.
5. Place a small fresh herb sprig in each jar. Fill with jelly to within ¼ inch of rim. Wipe rims with a clean cloth, cover with vacuum lid, and secure with metal ring. Load jars into canning kettle half filled with hot water. Add water to reach at least 2 inches above jar tops. Bring water to a boil and boil gently for 10 minutes. Remove jars; cool completely. Store up to 1 year in a cool, dark place.

Herb Jelly Variations

You can customize your herb jelly in a variety of ways. Use the basic jelly recipe on page 16 as your starting point and try one of the following variations. As you gain confidence, you'll come up with any number of creative new recipes.

- Use fruit juice for the herb infusion (step 2), instead of the 2 cups of water.
- Replace the 2½ cups apple juice with other unsweetened liquids like apple cider, white grape juice, grapefruit juice, or cranberry juice.
- Use lemon juice in place of the cider vinegar, depending on the flavor of the herb.

Here are some suggestions for combinations of herbs and juices to get you started. (Use the same amounts of sugar and Sure-Gel or other low-sugar pectin as specified by the basic recipe.)

HERB	LIQUID (WATER/JUICE)	VINEGAR/LEMON JUICE
2 cups mint leaves	2 cups boiling water and 2½ cups apple juice	4 tablespoons cider vinegar
2 cups basil leaves (cinnamon and holy basil, for instance)	2 cups boiling water and 2½ cups apple juice	4 tablespoons vinegar
1 cup sage leaves	2 cups boiling water and 2½ cups apple cider	4 tablespoons vinegar
1 cup savory leaves	4½ cups grapefruit juice	(none needed)
1 cup lemongrass stalks, plus ½ cup shredded coconut	4½ cups water	4 tablespoons lemon juice
1 cup rose-scented geranium leaves	2 cups boiling water and 2½ cups apple or white grape juice	4 tablespoons lemon juice
1 cup rosemary leaves, plus 2 cinnamon sticks and 6 whole cloves	4½ cups cranberry juice	(none needed)
¼ cup lemon verbena leaves	4½ cups water	4 tablespoons lemon juice

Rosemary-Goldenrod Jelly

Capture the golden sun of autumn with Goldenrod Jelly. Infuse 2 cups of packed fresh goldenrod (*Solidago* species) flowers, then follow the herb jelly directions on page 16. Infuse several sprigs of fresh rosemary in the hot jelly before bottling.

HERB HONEYS

Herb honeys are a snap to make. You can brew a batch with dried herbs any time of year. You'll also need unpasteurized honey, available from health-food stores or a local beekeeper. Choose the milder, light-colored honeys to give the herb flavor top billing. For herb flavorings, cinnamon basil leaves and flowering tops, lavender buds, rosemary leaves, chamomile flowers, rose-scented geranium leaves and flowers, and fragrant dianthus (carnations or clove pinks) flowers are my favorites.

Try this method with any herb combinations that appeal to you. The only rule is that you must use dried plant material because excess water from fresh herbs could dilute the honey enough to promote the growth of bacteria.

Use herb honeys in any recipe calling for honey and, of course, to sweeten herb tea. For a sweet spread for biscuits, whip a little herb honey into softened butter.

Safety first: *Use unsprayed herbs and flowers only!*

BASIC HONEY

¼ cup dried herbs
1 cup honey

1. Place the dried herbs in a sterilized glass jar. Cover with honey. Cap the jar tightly and let it sit in a cool, dark place for two weeks.
2. Strain the honey through a sieve and rebottle it. (If the honey is thick, heat it slightly in a pan of hot water to make straining easier.)

CHAPTER 2

DELICIOUS SEASONAL HERBAL
Recipes

If you're looking for a fresh idea in cooking, herbs are the answer. They bring incomparable taste and texture to your plate. And because herbs enhance foods' natural flavors, they can easily take the place of unhealthy ingredients such as fat and salt. Fresh rosemary, for example, adds an absolute flavor explosion to even the driest, most boring white fish. If you're growing your own herbs, make sure to keep them near the kitchen, where they'll be easily accessible. Let all your great meals begin in the garden!

Spring Recipes

Infant seedlings rouse to the warming rays of the sun. Hopeful patches of chervil and cilantro appear, eager green shoots of fragrant mint push through the surface of the mellow earth, chickweed billows over the cold frame, and here and there dandelions and violets unfurl their blooms. It's spring! Every breath of new life is cause for rejoicing — at least for now.

We never say spring is on time; it's either early or late. Technically, spring begins on the vernal equinox. For me, spring is official with the first salad of tender lettuce garnished with chervil and strewn with violet blossoms, served with surprisingly meaty Dandy Burgers (page 24) made from — you guessed it — dandelion blossoms!

Roasted Asparagus with Chervil and Violets
Serves 4–6

When I first heard mention of roasted asparagus, I was aghast. Frizzle fresh asparagus? I tried it, though — delicious! This is easy, elegant appetizer fare, served hot or cold. For this recipe, thick asparagus stalks work best.

Edible Spring Flowers

Tulips are edible and tasty, too — just ask the deer, which can eliminate an entire tulip bed in one meal, much to a gardener's dismay! Separate the petals from a few flowers and dab them with egg salad for an appetizer or with lemon curd for dessert. Other tasty spring herb flowers include pansies, chives, carnations, lavender, roses, thyme, borage, bergamot, dandelions, sweet woodruff, elderflowers, and calendulas. Eat only unsprayed posies that you can positively identify. Avoid blossoms from the florist, which most likely have been sprayed.

Lavender and rose petals

Household Herbs

1 pound asparagus stalks, trimmed
2 tablespoons olive oil
Coarse sea salt
Lemon juice
Fresh chervil and violet blossoms, minced, for garnish

1. Preheat oven to 450°F.
2. Place the asparagus in a heavy roasting pan, or spread it on a baking sheet. Drizzle the olive oil over the asparagus, then turn to coat. Sprinkle lightly with salt. Bake 10 to 15 minutes, or until asparagus is soft.
3. To serve, arrange asparagus on a platter, squeeze a little lemon juice over it, and garnish with minced chervil and violet blossoms.

Slimming Miso Soup
Serves 4

Miso soup is one of the gentlest ways to transition your body from traditionally heavy winter foods to lighter spring fare. And if like me at this time of the year you want to shed a few pounds before even considering a bathing suit, miso soup makes a nourishing, satisfying meal, whether for breakfast, lunch, or dinner. Miso soup is also an excellent choice for anyone convalescing from illness.

1 package (8.8 ounces) soba noodles
1 tablespoon raw sesame seeds
1 teaspoon roasted sesame oil
2 medium carrots, cut into ⅛-inch rounds
1 tablespoon grated raw gingerroot
⅓ cup thinly sliced shiitake mushrooms
6 cups water (use the drained cooking water from the noodles)
1 strip (3 inches) kombu seaweed, cut into slivers
6 scallions, slivered, with a little of the green
1 cup diced tofu
½ cup barley miso (available at natural food stores)
½ cup minced garlic chives

1. Cook the noodles according to package directions. Drain, reserving 6 cups of the cooking water.
2. Dry-toast the sesame seeds in a small, cast-iron skillet over low heat until fragrant. Reserve.
3. Heat the sesame oil in a large saucepan over medium heat. Sauté the carrots for 1 to 2 minutes, then stir in the gingerroot and mushrooms, and sauté 1 minute longer.
4. Add the water and seaweed. Stir. Bring the soup to a boil and adjust the heat to simmering. Cover, then cook for 10 minutes, or until the carrots are tender but not mushy.
5. Remove 1 cup of the broth and place in a small bowl. Add the scallions and tofu to the soup so they will warm through.
6. Stir the miso into the small bowl of broth, then combine the miso mixture with the soup.
7. Fill each bowl half full with noodles. Sprinkle the noodles with the garlic chives. Ladle the hot soup over the noodles and chives. Garnish with sesame seeds and serve immediately.

Lettuce and Lovage Soup

Serves 4

On a cool spring evening, a quick soup makes a satisfying meal, especially when served with fresh warm bread or biscuits, topped with parsley and chive or tarragon herb butter (see page 11).

5 cups chicken or vegetable stock
2 red potatoes, scrubbed (but not peeled) and grated
1 medium leek, white and tender green parts only, cut into thin rounds
1 head leaf lettuce, shredded
½ cup chopped lovage (leaves and stems)
¼ cup chopped fresh flat-leaf parsley
1 tablespoon chopped fresh mint
1 tablespoon chopped fresh dill
1 tablespoon chopped fresh tarragon
Salt and freshly ground black pepper, to taste
Herb butter (see page 13)
Calendula petals, for garnish (optional)

Parsley

1. In a large pot, heat the chicken or vegetable stock to boiling. Add the potatoes, leek, and lettuce, and cook for 10 minutes over medium heat or until the vegetables are soft.
2. Stir in the chopped herbs. Cover the pot, remove from heat, and let sit for 5 minutes.
3. Return the soup to a simmer. Season with salt and pepper, and serve immediately with a dab of herb butter and calendula petals.

Cilantro Pesto Pizza
Serves 2 (4 medium-size pieces)

Here's a great way to use the cilantro before it bolts. Pesto is a sauce made with an herb (usually basil) and garlic, oil, nuts, and cheese. This cilantro pesto tops a pizza. Serve with a salad for a light repast, or cut the pizza into small pieces for appetizers.

- 2 cups packed fresh cilantro (leaves and tender stems)
- 1–2 coarsely chopped jalapeño peppers
- 3–4 cloves garlic, finely minced
- ½ teaspoon salt
- ¼ cup fruity extra-virgin olive oil
- ¼ cup ricotta cheese
- 1 unbaked pizza shell (10 inches)
- Freshly ground black pepper
- ½ cup grated Parmesan or pecorino cheese
- 1 cup grated mozzarella cheese

1. Preheat oven to 425°F.
2. Place the cilantro, peppers, garlic, and salt in a food processor. Process until evenly ground. With the motor running, pour in the olive oil in a thin stream. Process until pureed. Add the ricotta cheese and process just until blended.
3. Spread the pesto on the pizza shell. Add a few grinds of pepper, then spread the Parmesan or pecorino and the mozzarella on top.
4. Bake for 12 to 15 minutes, or until bubbly and golden. Serve immediately.

Pasta with Cilantro Pesto

Cilantro pesto is also wonderful over pasta: Thin the herb/pepper/garlic puree on page 23 with enough extra-virgin olive oil to make a sauce. Or, to reduce calories, use some of the pasta cooking water and less oil to thin the puree.

Dandy Burgers

SERVES 2 (4 MEDIUM-SIZE BURGERS)

Although some see dandelions as irritating weeds rather than sunny blossoms lighting up their lawns, anyone can enjoy dandelion burgers. Believe it or not, these tasty patties remind me of crab cakes, especially when served with cocktail sauce. Come on, give it a try. (Of course, never eat anything from a lawn that has been sprayed with chemicals.)

- 2 cups packed freshly opened dandelion blossoms
- 1 cup crumbled saltine or Ritz crackers
- ½ cup finely chopped onion
- 2 tablespoons Dijon mustard
- 2 tablespoons finely minced flat-leaved parsley
- Dash Tabasco sauce
- Salt and freshly ground black pepper, to taste
- 1 egg, well beaten
- 1 tablespoon safflower oil or butter, for frying
- Cocktail sauce (optional)

1. To prepare the dandelion flowers, trim off all the bitter green stems with scissors. Cut the blossoms into quarters. Mix the trimmed blossoms with the remaining ingredients, except cocktail sauce.
2. Shape into patties.
3. Fry over medium heat until golden brown on both sides, about 8 minutes in total. Serve hot, with cocktail sauce if desired.

Dandelion

Watercress Salad with Citrus Dressing

Serves 4

This is a refreshing spring salad for a low-calorie, high-energy lunch.

- 1 tablespoon chopped walnuts
- 1 bunch watercress, torn into small pieces
- 2 hard-cooked eggs, sliced
- 3 tablespoons fresh orange juice
- 2 tablespoons fresh lemon juice
- 1 teaspoon roasted sesame oil
- 1/3 cup walnut oil
- Freshly ground black pepper, to taste
- 2 tablespoons finely minced fresh chervil or cilantro

1. Dry-toast the walnuts in a small cast-iron skillet. Reserve.
2. Place the watercress on individual salad plates, and arrange the egg slices on top.
3. Whisk the juices and oils in a small bowl. Drizzle over the salad.
4. Add pepper, and garnish with the minced chervil or cilantro.

Floral Salad Plates

Try this special presentation for Mother's Day or any special spring celebration. You'll need two salad plates for each serving — they'll be stacked on top of each other. The top plate should be a little smaller and must be glass or crystal; the bottom plate can be glass or a solid color. On the larger bottom plate, arrange a pretty pattern of green leaves and colorful flowers, such as dill, pansies, flat-leaved parsley, chives, carnations, and bergamot. For the top plate, prepare your favorite mixed-green salad. Set the plate of salad over the larger plate. As the salad is eaten, the flower plate will be revealed!

Delicious Seasonal Herbal Recipes

Pasta with Field Greens and Basil-Peanut Sauce

Serves 4–6

Fragrant and rich, this dish is perfect for a day when you've expended many calories digging in the herb garden! Before heading toward the kitchen, cut field greens like dandelions, chicory, and cress, or garden vegetables like bok choy, collards, mizuna, endive, watercress, and arugula. (Don't cook the watercress or arugula — they'll wilt enough when tossed with hot noodles and sauce.) Any leftover sauce makes wonderful dressing for a salad of watercress, sliced chicken, oranges, snow peas, and scallions.

For the Basil-Peanut Sauce
- 1½ cups unsalted roasted peanuts
- 2–3 cloves garlic, finely minced
- 1-inch slice fresh gingerroot, cut into chunks
- 2 tablespoons tamari or soy sauce
- 1 teaspoon roasted sesame oil
- 1 scant tablespoon frozen basil puree (see page 116), or 2 tablespoons fresh basil
- Pinch of cayenne pepper
- Juice of 1 lime
- 1 tablespoon orange juice concentrate

For the Pasta
- 1 pound linguine
- 1 tablespoon herb vinegar, such as Opal Basil-Garlic-Black Peppercorn (page 118) or nasturtium flower vinegar
- 2 cups julienned mixed field greens
- ½ cup scallions, cut into small rounds

1. Place all the Basil-Peanut Sauce ingredients in a food processor. Process until almost smooth — a few chunks are nice.
2. Meanwhile, cook pasta according to package directions, adding a tablespoon of herb vinegar to the cooking water. Add the julienned greens to the boiling pasta about 2 minutes before the pasta is done.
3. Allow the water to return to a boil, cook for 1 minute, then drain, reserving about ½ cup of the water to thin the sauce.
4. Dress the hot pasta with the peanut sauce and scallions, adding some of the reserved cooking water if needed.

Household Herbs

Roasted Scallions

Serves 4–6

Serve this delicious side dish with meats, chicken, or grilled fish. If you're grilling, toss scallions with oil and put them on the grill during the last 3 to 5 minutes of cooking the entree. Turn once.

> 24 scallions
> Extra-virgin olive oil
> Juice of 1 lemon
> Salt and freshly ground black pepper, to taste
> Finely minced chervil, parsley, or cilantro, for garnish

1. Preheat oven to 475°F.
2. Trim the root end and the tough part of the green stalks from the scallions. Arrange the scallions in a single layer on a baking sheet. Drizzle them lightly with olive oil, turning to coat evenly.
3. Roast scallions 15 to 20 minutes, turning once or twice, until they are tender and lightly browned. Remove them from the oven.
4. Arrange scallions on a serving dish and sprinkle with lemon juice. Season with salt and pepper. Garnish with freshly minced herbs.

Herb-Dyed Easter Eggs

Natural-dyed eggs are beautiful in baskets and table arrangements. Fill a large saucepan with leaves or vegetable skins (see below). Cover with water, and boil for 10 minutes. Add the eggs and boil 5 minutes more. Remove from heat and cover the pot until cool. If you plan to eat the eggs, refrigerate them as soon as they're cool. If you are using them only for decoration, you can let them sit in the dye water for several hours or overnight.
Herbs to Try: Sage or nettle greens for khaki brown; dandelion blossoms for bright yellow; ground turmeric (2 teaspoons per cup water) for gold; onion skins for mahogany; red cabbage leaves plus 1 tablespoon vinegar for purplish blue; red beets plus 1 tablespoon vinegar for pink.

Poached Salmon with Dill Yogurt Sauce
Serves 4

An easy, festive dish that's delicious hot or cold. Serve it with Roasted Vegetable Treats (page 42) and a fresh green salad for a simple-to-make company meal.

For the Dill Yogurt Sauce
- 1 tablespoon unsalted butter
- 2 shallots, finely minced
- 2 tablespoons finely chopped fresh dill
- 1 tablespoon finely chopped fresh chervil
- 1 tablespoon capers
- 1 teaspoon fresh lemon juice
- 1/8 teaspoon white pepper
- 1 cup plain nonfat yogurt

For the Poached Salmon
- 6 cups water
- 2 cups unsweetened apple or white grape juice
- 6 stalks lemongrass
- 2 cloves garlic, peeled and halved
- 1/2 cup sliced scallions
- 1/2 cup fresh parsley
- 2 bay leaves
- 2 pounds thick salmon fillets, cut into four equal pieces

1. For the Dill Yogurt Sauce, heat butter in small saucepan over medium-low heat. Sauté the shallots until they are golden brown. Remove pan from the heat.
2. Combine the butter and shallots with the remaining ingredients in a small bowl. Heat until warm (do not boil) if serving with hot fish, or chill for use with cold fish.
3. Place the water, apple or grape juice, lemongrass, garlic, scallions, parsley, and bay leaves in a large saucepan or fish poacher. Bring to a boil, then reduce heat and simmer for 10 minutes.
4. Slide the salmon into the hot liquid. Adjust heat until there is a slight ripple of water bubbling over the fish. Cover. Cook 8 to 10 minutes.
5. Carefully remove the salmon from the pan and arrange it on a platter. Serve hot or chilled with Dill Yogurt Sauce.

Dill

Uncle Bicky's Not-Red Barbecued Chicken

Serves 6–8

When the first warm weekend rolls into town, it's time to make iced tea and fire up the grill for the best barbecued chicken you've ever eaten. This is not your sticky-sweet red barbecue sauce, but a tangy concoction as flavorful as my Eastern Shore kin. It's delicious hot or cold.

- ¼ cup kosher salt
- 1 teaspoon freshly ground black pepper
- 3 tablespoons Poultry Seasoning (page 10)
- 1½ cups apple cider vinegar
- 1 egg
- 2 fryer chickens, cut into pieces

1. Place the salt and pepper, Poultry Seasoning, vinegar, and egg in a blender, and whiz for 30 seconds or until well combined.
2. Place the chicken pieces in zipper-lock plastic bags or a large bowl and cover with sauce, reserving ¼ cup for basting. Marinate in the refrigerator for several hours, turning occasionally to coat evenly.
3. Grill chicken pieces until they're done, about 20 to 45 minutes, depending on size of chicken pieces and amount of heat in coals. Baste with reserved marinade for the first 5 minutes of cooking.

An Herbal Basting Brush

A branch of rosemary or sage makes a flavorful (and compostable!) brush for basting vegetables and meats on the grill. Bundle several together, mixing "flavors" if you wish, and tie them with raffia. Give one as a gift, with one of your favorite grilling recipes and a jar of savory herb jelly tucked into the package.

Summer Recipes

Summer menus sing a lighthearted song of sweet basil and tomatoes, and fresh summer vegetables and fruits need little fancy fixing. Who wants to stay in the kitchen anyway? Enjoy these seasonal foods enhanced with cooling herbs like basil, marjoram, dill, and savory or, alternatively, pumped so high with hot chilies that sweltering August temperatures feel cool by comparison. Even if you don't have a garden, farm stands provide abundant harvests, so fill your gathering basket and support your local growers. We've waited all year, and summer is finally here!

Broiled Pesto Vegetable Rounds

SERVES 6–8 AS APPETIZERS

Leftover pesto or frozen herb paste (see page 151) makes this quick appetizer especially easy to make. I like to arrange three whole pumpkin seeds on each vegetable round. The pesto is also good spread on baguette slices and broiled for quick toasts to serve as appetizers with soup. Any leftover pesto will keep in the refrigerator for at least two weeks. Pour a thin film of olive oil over the pesto to prevent discoloration.

For the Pesto

- ¼ cup packed fresh summer savory leaves
- ¾ cup fresh Italian parsley leaves
- 2 tablespoons extra-virgin olive oil
- 1–2 minced garlic cloves
- 1 tablespoon lemon juice
- Pinch of salt

For the Vegetables

- 12 new potatoes, scrubbed and cut in half
- 2 summer squash, cut in ¼-inch rounds
- ⅓–½ cup pumpkin seeds, walnuts, sunflower seeds, or pine nuts, for topping
- Parmesan cheese
- Freshly ground black pepper, to taste

1. Chop the herbs in a food processor or blender. With the motor running, pour in the olive oil in a thin stream. Add the remaining pesto ingredients and blend until smooth. Set aside.

2. Steam potatoes for 5 minutes to partially cook them.
3. Set the broiler rack 6 inches from the source of heat, and turn on the broiler.
4. Cover a cookie sheet with aluminum foil and spray it with nonstick cooking spray.
5. Lay the vegetables in a single layer on the cookie sheet. Use a tablespoon to spread them with a thin coating of pesto. Arrange the seeds or nuts on top, and finish with a sprinkle of Parmesan cheese.
6. Broil until the topping is sizzling, about 3 to 5 minutes. Season with pepper to taste, and serve immediately.

Orange and Red Tomato Salsa with Cilantro

Makes 2–3 cups

American taste is changing: Salsa now outsells ketchup! This is a basic recipe — you can add diced tomatillos, sweet peppers, and/or cucumbers. The sweeter flavor of orange tomatoes adds a delicious and colorful touch, but don't worry if you can't find any. Meaty Italian tomatoes like Romas make a thicker salsa. If your tomatoes are juicy, strain out some of the liquid before adding the remaining ingredients. Out of cilantro? Use chopped basil or other salsa herbs (see page 32). Serve salsa as a dip with chips or as a topping for burgers, fajitas, or open-faced grilled cheese sandwiches. Salsa is also delicious on pizza.

- 1 red tomato, skinned and cubed
- 1 orange tomato, skinned and cubed
- 2 tablespoons finely minced red or Vidalia onion
- ½ cup finely minced fresh cilantro, plus extra for garnish
- 1 tablespoon fresh lime juice
- 1 tablespoon finely minced jalapeño pepper (dragon-breath types can use more!)

1. Mix together all ingredients in a small bowl. Use immediately, or refrigerate until serving time.
2. To serve, garnish with additional cilantro if desired.

Other Salsa Herbs

When hot summertime weather hits, cilantro withers. Try growing papalo (*Porophyllum ruderale* spp. *macrocephalum*) from Mexico and quillquina (*Porophyllum ruderale*) from Bolivia, two salsa herbs that can really take the heat. Both of these herbs have stronger flavors than that of cilantro, so use half as much as a recipe calls for, and taste before adding more.

Tomato Tarragon Soup
Makes about 2 quarts

An easy, elegant dish, Tomato Tarragon Soup can be made even prettier if you ladle it into individual bowls and swirl in a little plain yogurt thinned with a teaspoon of tarragon vinegar. Garnish with a few leaves of fresh tarragon and calendula petals. If there's no fresh gingerroot on hand, substitute 1 teaspoon powdered ginger when adding the tarragon. Black-Skillet Corn Bread (page 39) is a nice complement to this dish.

- 2 tablespoons extra-virgin olive oil
- 1 tablespoon butter
- 1 cup diced shallots
- 1 tablespoon grated fresh gingerroot
- 5 pounds red ripe tomatoes, peeled and cut into large pieces
- 1 teaspoon salt
- 2 tablespoons fresh tarragon, minced
- Salt and freshly ground black pepper, to taste

1. Heat the oil and butter in a large saucepan over medium-low heat. Add the shallots and gingerroot, and sauté for a few minutes until shallots soften.

Tarragon

Household Herbs

2. Add the tomatoes and salt. Cover, bring to a boil, then lower heat and simmer gently for 1 hour. Check occasionally to make sure there is enough liquid.
3. Add the tarragon and cook for 20 minutes more.
4. Cool for 30 mintues. Puree in the blender. If desired, pass the puree through a food mill to remove seeds. Season with salt and pepper to taste. Serve hot or cold.

Green Beans with Garlic and Savory

S E R V E S 4

When green beans are abundant, steam enough for several meals, undercooking them slightly. At mealtime, stir-fry them in a nonstick skillet. Try this same recipe with fresh summer squash cut into small strips.

- 1 pound green beans, trimmed
- 1 tablespoon olive oil
- 2 cloves garlic, minced
- 1 tablespoon minced fresh savory, for garnish

1. Steam the green beans for 5 minutes. They should still be crisp. Refrigerate them until you're ready to serve.
2. Heat the olive oil in a skillet over medium-low heat. Sauté the garlic briefly until it begins to turn golden. Add the beans and toss until heated through. Serve garnished with the fresh savory.

Zucchini Fritters with Cheese and Basil

S E R V E S 4

An easy, satisfying meal for any time of day, these fritters are good with applesauce. Arrowhead Mills makes a terrific multigrain pancake mix; you may find it at your local natural-foods store.

- 1 pound zucchini, grated (about 3 cups)
- ¼ cup finely minced onion
- ¼ teaspoon salt
- 2 tablespoons finely minced fresh basil

    ¾ cup pancake mix
⅓ cup finely chopped walnuts
½ cup grated cheddar cheese
½ cup skim milk
  1 large egg, well beaten
   Scant tablespoon canola oil for the pan

1. Place the grated zucchini and the onion in a sieve. Sprinkle with the salt and let stand 10 minutes. Squeeze to extract excess liquid, then place in a medium-size bowl.
2. Combine the basil, pancake mix, walnuts, and grated cheese in a small bowl.
3. Combine the milk and beaten egg, and stir into the zucchini mixture. Add the pancake mixture and stir until just combined.
4. Heat a small amount of canola oil in a nonstick frying pan over medium heat. Fry fritters, turning once, until cooked through and golden brown on both sides.

Summer Pizza with Zucchini, Provolone, Feta, and Artichoke Hearts

MAKES 4 MEDIUM-SIZE PIECES

With ready-made flatbreads for the crust, this delicious dinner can be prepared in minutes. The flatbread I like best is made by Garden of Eatin. Flatbreads freeze well and are handy to have on reserve for emergency appetizers.

  1 flatbread (8 x 11 inches)
¼ pound provolone cheese, thinly sliced
  2 medium zucchini, cut lengthwise into very thin slices
  1 cup canned artichoke hearts, drained and cut into small pieces
  1 small Vidalia onion, finely sliced
  1 tablespoon minced fresh marjoram
   Freshly ground black pepper, to taste
½ cup crumbled feta cheese

1. Preheat the oven to 475°F. Spray a cookie sheet with nonstick cooking spray.

2. Place the flatbread on the cookie sheet. Cover the flatbread with the provolone cheese, then layer on the zucchini. Sprinkle with the artichokes, onion, marjoram, and pepper. Top with the feta cheese.
3. Bake for 8 to 10 minutes, or until golden brown.

Mexican Chicken Salad
Serves 6

Great for a summer picnic, this chicken salad is wonderful paired with a plate of sliced tomatoes sprinkled with basil, olive oil and vinegar, and salt and pepper to taste. Barely cooked corn cut fresh from the cob makes a wonderful accompaniment to this recipe. For another fresh touch, grind your own cumin: Simply toast cumin seeds in a heavy skillet over medium-low heat until they are fragrant, then grind them using a mortar and pestle. If you'd like to try a vegetarian variation of this same recipe, it's very tasty made with marinated or baked tofu instead of the chicken breast. Add chopped tomatoes and sweet peppers if you like.

1½ pounds boneless, skinless chicken breast
1 can (15 ounces) black beans, drained
1½ cups corn
2 tablespoons olive oil
3 cloves garlic, finely minced
½ cup diced scallions
½ cup finely minced parsley or cilantro
1 tablespoon finely minced fresh marjoram
1½ teaspoons ground cumin
2 tablespoons rice or white wine vinegar
½ teaspoon salt or 1 teaspoon Cajun Blend (page 11)

Marjoram

1. Place the chicken breasts in a medium-size skillet or saucepan. Add enough boiling water to cover. Bring water to a simmer, then cook over low heat, turning once. Cook until just done, about 4 minutes on each side. Drain and cool.
2. Cut cooked chicken into cubes, and place them in a large bowl. Add the remaining ingredients and mix well. Chill until serving time.

Baked Fish Steaks with Lemon Thyme

S E R V E S 4

Even folks who claim they don't like fish enjoy this dish, especially with basmati rice. Mako shark is a good choice if you like fish, or substitute pressed tofu if you wish.

> 2 pounds fresh fish steaks
> 1 tablespoon plain nonfat yogurt
> 1 tablespoon lemon zest
> 1 tablespoon finely minced lemon thyme
> ½ cup unsweetened apple or white grape juice

1. Preheat the oven to 450°F. Line a baking sheet with heavy-duty aluminum foil, using a piece large enough to wrap and seal the fish.
2. Place the fish on the foil, and brush it with the yogurt. Mix the lemon zest and herbs in a small bowl. Sprinkle the herb mixture over the fish. Bring the foil up around the fish. Pour the fruit juice around the fish, then seal the foil over the fish.
3. Bake for 20 minutes. Test for doneness: The fish should be cooked through, but still slightly pink inside. Serve piping hot.

Center-Stage Herbs

Don't forget to feature the complementary colors and fragrances of fresh herbs when you make flower arrangements. Try floating flower blossoms, such as pansies, chamomile, and roses, in shallow crystal bowls of water. It's fun to see the flower faces "up close and personal," and the effect is very cooling, as well.

For gathered arrangements, try orange mint with daisies; nasturtium leaves and flowers; spires of bergamot, lavender, or salvia; or sprays of sunny gold calendulas — perfect with opal basil!

Lemony Shrimp with Pasta
SERVES 4

Here's a festive dish that looks as though you spent hours in the kitchen. The only time-consuming step is peeling the shrimp. Buy a half-dozen extra with which to bribe the sous-chef!

For the Marinade
- Juice of 1 lemon
- 1 tablespoon olive oil
- 2 tablespoons finely minced rosemary
- 2 garlic cloves, minced
- ½ teaspoon salt
- ⅛ teaspoon cayenne powder
- 1 pound peeled fresh shrimp

For the Pasta
- 1 pound linguine
- 6 stalks lemongrass
- ¼ cup extra-virgin olive oil
- Zest and juice of 1 lemon
- ½–¾ cup Parmesan cheese
- ¼ cup finely minced fresh parsley
- Freshly ground black pepper, to taste

1. Combine all the marinade ingredients (except the shrimp) in a medium-size bowl. Add the shrimp and mix well to coat.
2. Refrigerate shrimp for at least 30 minutes, or up to 8 hours.
3. Heat a nonstick skillet over medium-high heat. Toss the shrimp in the marinade to coat thoroughly, strain out most of the marinade, and sauté for 4 to 5 minutes.
4. Cook the pasta with the lemongrass until the pasta is done. Discard the lemongrass, but reserve ½ cup of the cooking liquid.
5. Toss the pasta with the remaining ingredients and cooked shrimp, adding a little of the reserved cooking water from the pasta if needed. Serve immediately.

Fettucine with Garlicky Zucchini
Serves 4

Many summer vegetables work well in this quick from-the-garden pasta dish. Instead of the zucchini, try julienned carrots, kohlrabi, green beans, or eggplant. Arugula and radicchio are also wonderful in it; shred the raw vegetables or use leftovers, stir-frying them briefly with the garlic to reheat. Substitute pumpkin seeds or pine nuts for the walnuts if you'd like.

- 1 pound zucchini, cut into 2-inch julienne strips
- ¼ cup olive oil
- 6–8 garlic cloves, finely minced
- ¾ pound fettucine
- 3 tablespoons finely minced fresh parsley
- 3 tablespoons finely minced garlic chives
- 2 tablespoons finely minced marjoram
- 1 tablespoon lemon juice or herb vinegar
- ½ cup grated Parmesan cheese, plus additional for topping
- ⅓ cup chopped English walnuts, toasted
- Freshly ground black pepper, to taste

1. Steam the zucchini until just tender, 3 to 5 minutes. Reserve.
2. Heat the olive oil in a small, nonstick skillet over medium-low heat. Add the garlic and sauté until golden brown, being careful not to burn. Remove from heat.
3. Cook the pasta until al dente, then drain, reserving ½ cup of the cooking liquid.
4. Toss the pasta with the zucchini, garlic, herbs, lemon juice or vinegar, and grated cheese. Add a little of the reserved cooking water if needed to coat the pasta. Top with the toasted walnuts. Season with pepper, and serve with more grated cheese.

Garlic chives

Black-Skillet Corn Bread

Makes 4 generous pieces

An 8-inch cast-iron skillet is the secret weapon in this comforting dish of my grandfather's. If you don't have buttermilk, add 1 tablespoon of lemon juice or herb vinegar to nonfat milk to equal 1 cup.

- 1 cup buttermilk
- 1 egg
- 1 tablespoon maple syrup
- 1 cup white cornmeal
- 1 teaspoon baking soda
- 1 scant teaspoon salt
- 1 tablespoon coarsely chopped fresh marjoram
- 1 tablespoon butter

1. Preheat oven to 450°F.
2. Whisk together the buttermilk, egg, and syrup in a medium-size bowl until the egg is well beaten.
3. Measure the dry ingredients and the marjoram in another bowl, and stir to combine. Pour the cornmeal mix into the liquid mix, and whip lightly to combine.
4. When the oven is hot, put the butter in a skillet and place it in the oven. Set the timer for 2 or 3 minutes so you don't forget to remove the pan before the butter burns. Remove the skillet from the oven — the butter should be bubbling. (Use a heavy pot holder!) Immediately pour the batter into the skillet. Bake 15 to 20 minutes, or until corn bread is golden brown.

Pretty as a Picture

Many garden flowers and most herb blossoms make delightful edible garnishes. Safe and tasty choices include begonia, bergamot, borage, calendula, carnation, scented geraniums, hollyhocks, honeysuckle, 'Lemon Gem' marigolds, Mexican marigolds, nasturtiums, portulaca, rosemary, roses, scarlet runner bean, snapdragon, thyme, and yucca. Use small whole blossoms or petals from larger flowers. Use only unsprayed plants (not from florists).

Delicious Seasonal Herbal Recipes

One-Bowl Blueberry Cake

ONE 8-INCH SQUARE OR ROUND LAYER

Although this last-minute dessert doesn't need icing, it's delicious with Simple Orange Icing. Use chopped peaches instead of blueberries when they're in season.

- ¾ cup milk
- 5–6 lemon verbena leaves (fresh or dried) *or* 6 sprigs fresh lemon balm leaves
- 5 tablespoons softened, unsalted butter
- ¾ cup brown sugar
- 1 egg
- 1 teaspoon vanilla
- 1¾ cups unbleached flour
- 2 teaspoons baking soda
- ¼ teaspoon salt
- ¼ teaspoon ground nutmeg
- 1 cup fresh blueberries

1. Heat milk until it is hot but not boiling. Stir in whole lemon verbena leaves. Cover and let steep until milk reaches room temperature. Strain out herb leaves and discard. Reserve the milk.
2. Preheat the oven to 350°F. Grease and flour a cake pan.
3. In a medium-size bowl, cream butter and sugar. Beat in egg and vanilla.
4. Combine the dry ingredients in another bowl, and stir to mix. Add the flour mixture and milk alternately to the egg mixture, beginning and ending with the milk. Beat for a minute or two, or until smooth.
5. Fold in the blueberries. Turn the batter into the prepared pan.
6. Bake for 25 to 30 minutes, or until the cake tests done. Allow the cake to cool slightly in the pan for several minutes and then turn it onto a wire rack to cool. Frost if desired.

For Simple Orange Icing
- 1 tablespoon softened unsalted butter
- 1 tablespoon orange juice concentrate
- 1 cup confectioners' sugar

With an electric mixer, beat all ingredients until smooth. Icing should be thin. Spread on the cooled cake, allowing the icing to drizzle down the sides.

Autumn Recipes

Harvesttime: Market stands overflow with a carnival of pumpkins, winter squash, apples, garlic, sweet potatoes, and Indian corn. It's the last call for summer squash, tomatoes, and peppers — suddenly precious, now that chilling winds have crept through the fields. The scent of warm herbs wafts through the kitchen — rosemary, sage, thyme, and bay. Hardy cool-weather greens like parsley, cilantro, and chervil, and wildings like dandelions, cress, and chicory are making a fresh comeback. Now is the time to gather in the great energy of spring and summer represented in the garden vegetables, grains, and herbs that soaked up the sun's vitality. Properly stored and prepared, these potent gifts will warm us through the winter.

Rosemary-Roasted Jerusalem Artichokes

Serves 4

Jerusalem artichokes (also called sunchokes) thrive in some of the worst conditions, even in petrified clay soil. This recipe makes a finger-licking-good appetizer out of these indomitable plants. The only time-consuming job is scrubbing the tubers clean. If you don't have 'chokes, you can prepare sliced potatoes in the same manner with tasty results.

- 2 pounds unpeeled Jerusalem artichokes, cut into 2-inch pieces
- 1–2 tablespoons olive oil
- ¼ cup coarsely chopped fresh or dried rosemary
- 1 teaspoon salt

1. Preheat the oven to 425°F.
2. Mix the artichoke pieces with the olive oil. Spread the artichokes in a single layer on a baking sheet. Sprinkle with the rosemary and salt.
3. Bake 25 to 30 minutes, or until tender. Serve hot — with plenty of napkins.

Rosemary

Delicious Seasonal Herbal Recipes

Roasted Vegetable Treats

Roasted vegetables are hot! Cooking vegetables at a high temperature intensifies flavors, transforming ho-hum into yum. Resinous shrubby herbs like rosemary, sage, thyme, and bay are natural companions for vegetables. Use the recipe for Jerusalem artichokes to experiment with carrots, beets, parsnips, turnips, potatoes, Brussels sprouts, onions, and winter squash. No need to peel the vegetables — the skins hold in flavor.

Vary the herbs to your liking.

Savory Spaghetti Squash Salsa

MAKES 5 CUPS

Salsa lovers of all ages will enjoy this autumn twist! Kids like to scoop out the spaghetti-like strands of this easy-to-grow winter squash, which stores well all winter.

- 1 medium-size spaghetti squash
- 1 cup peeled and diced plum tomatoes (about 2–3)
- 1 can (15 ounces) black beans, rinsed and drained
- 2 cloves garlic, finely minced
- 1 jalapeño pepper, finely minced
- ¼ cup lime juice
- 1 tablespoon balsamic or herb vinegar
- 2 tablespoons minced fresh parsley
- 1 tablespoon minced fresh marjoram
- 1 teaspoon dried savory
- Pinch of sugar
- Pinch of cayenne pepper
- Salt and freshly ground black pepper, to taste

1. Preheat the oven to 350°F.
2. Cut squash in half lengthwise. Remove seeds. Place cut-sides down in a 9 × 13-inch baking dish. Add ½ inch of water to dish.
3. Bake for 45 minutes, or until the skin is tender to the touch. Cool.
4. Remove the flesh with a fork, and place it in a large mixing bowl. Add the remaining ingredients and combine well. Chill until serving time. Great with spicy corn chips.

Composed Autumn Salad

SERVES 4

The secret to cooking collards and kale is to julienne the greens so they cook quickly, retaining color and flavor but not toughness. Use a full-flavored vinegar for this dish — balsamic vinegar and seasoned rice vinegar are good choices. When layering the salad, I like to add a final flourish of grated radish, ginger, or apple. Serve at room temperature or slightly chilled.

1 pound collard or kale greens
Splash of apple cider vinegar
⅓ cup olive oil
1 teaspoon toasted sesame oil
1 tablespoon tamari
2 tablespoons vinegar
1 cup uncooked sauerkraut
⅓ cup minced garlic chives

Optional garnishes: grated ginger, grated apple, grated radish, pomegranate seeds, halved black or red grapes, dried cranberries (soak first in sauerkraut juice to soften), toasted walnuts, pumpkin seeds, or other nuts

1. Wash the greens and strip the leafy parts from the tough inner stems. Roll the leaves lengthwise into long cigars. Using a sharp knife, cut the leaves crosswise into thin strips.
2. Bring a large pot of water to a boil. Add the julienned greens, stirring to submerge all of the leaves. Add a splash of vinegar. Return the water to boiling, uncovered, and set the timer for 5 minutes.

Spicy Squash Seeds

Toast the seeds of any winter squash for a healthy snack. To prepare, separate the seeds from the fiber and wash clean. Drain. Spread the seeds on a greased baking sheet. Drizzle with a little olive oil and turn to coat. Sprinkle with salt or Cajun Blend (page 11). Bake in a 400°F oven for 20 minutes, or until golden brown, shaking the pan occasionally. Squash seeds keep better raw than toasted, so wait to toast them until you plan to use them.

3. When the buzzer rings, taste-test the greens to make sure they're tender. Cook for a minute or two longer if necessary, but don't let them get mushy.
4. Pour the greens into a colander. Run cold water over them until they are cool to the touch. Let drain.
5. Put the oils, tamari, and 2 tablespoons of vinegar in a glass jar with a tight-fitting, nonmetal lid. When ready to serve, shake the dressing until it is well blended.
6. Compose the salad: first a layer of cooked greens, then a layer of sauerkraut; sprinkle the garlic chives and pour dressing to taste. Add optional garnish if desired.

Curried Sweet Potato Soup

Serves 6–8

Here's a golden autumn recipe: calcium-rich sweet potatoes warmed with nourishing ginger, sage, and curry. Once you roast the sweet potatoes, the soup is ready to eat in 20 minutes. This is my family's favorite first course for Thanksgiving dinner. With crusty bread and a salad, this soup makes a hearty meal.

- 3 medium-to-large sweet potatoes
- 1 tablespoon olive oil, plus a little to rub on potatoes
- 1 Spanish onion, finely minced
- 1 teaspoon to 2 tablespoons prepared Indian curry paste, to taste
- 3 sage leaves, fresh or dried
- 2 tablespoons unsweetened coconut
- 1 tablespoon grated fresh ginger
- 1 tablespoon curry powder
- 4 cups water
- 2½ cups apple cider
- Dollop of vanilla yogurt, for garnish

1. Preheat the oven to 425°F.
2. Scrub the sweet potatoes and rub them lightly with some olive oil. Place the potatoes on a rack in a roasting pan and bake for 45 minutes, or until soft. Cool and peel the potatoes.

3. Place a stockpot over medium heat. Add the rest of the olive oil. Sauté the minced onion in the hot oil until softened. Stir in the curry paste, sage leaves, coconut, ginger, and curry powder. Sauté for a few minutes to blend the flavors.
4. Add the meat from the peeled sweet potatoes. Sauté briefly. Stir in the water and apple cider. Reduce heat to low and simmer for 15 to 20 minutes.
5. Puree the soup in a blender before serving. A dollop of vanilla yogurt makes a cooling garnish. For a pretty spiderweb effect, thin the yogurt with a little apple cider, drizzle it in a spiral into each bowl, then use a table knife to cut through the spirals.

Spicy Black Bean Turkey Chili with Winter Squash

SERVES 8

On a frosty fall night, this chili is rapturous paired with corn bread. Dried chipotles are worth keeping on hand for any southwestern-style bean dish. Many grocery stores keep them in stock, but if you can't find them, feel free to use another type of hot pepper, fresh or dried. One small butternut squash yields about 6 cups of diced flesh. If you have any frozen sweet corn, try adding a cup in the last few minutes of cooking. I like to ladle the soup over torn arugula greens to make a one-bowl meal.

- 1 teaspoon cumin seeds
- 2–3 jalapeño peppers, peeled and chopped
- 1 red bell pepper, peeled and chopped
- 2 tablespoons canola oil
- 6–8 cloves garlic, finely minced
- 1 large Spanish onion, chopped
- 1 pound ground turkey
- 1½ cups vegetable stock
- 6 cups peeled and cubed butternut squash
- 1 dried chipotle chili (optional)
- 1 tablespoon minced fresh sage
- 1 can black beans, rinsed and drained
- 4 tablespoons red wine vinegar, such as Opal Basil-Garlic-Black Peppercorn Vinegar (page 118) (optional)

1. Toast the cumin seeds over low heat in a small cast-iron skillet. Grind them with a mortar and pestle and reserve.
2. Roast and peel the peppers (see page 70). Reserve.
3. Heat the oil in a large saucepan over medium-low heat. Add the

garlic, sauté for 1 minute, then add the onion and continue to sauté until the onion begins to soften.
4. Stir in the turkey and sauté until lightly browned.
5. Add stock, cubed squash, roasted peppers, and the optional chipotle chili. Cover and cook for 30 minutes.
6. Add the sage and drained beans. Cook 15 minutes more, or until the squash is tender. Add a splash of vinegar (about ½ tablespoon) to each bowl before serving if desired.

Roasted Pepper Pitas
Serves 4

Enjoy roasted red peppers in a pita sandwich, or marinate them in Autumn Walnut Vinaigrette and use as a topping for pizza, pasta, salads, or sandwiches.

- 2 tablespoons coarsely chopped walnuts
- 4 regular or onion pitas
- 1 cup chopped Rosemary-Roasted Peppers (page 47)
- ½ cup crumbled feta cheese
- 1 teaspoon dried marjoram
- A few arugula or watercress leaves
- ½ cup thinly sliced cucumbers
- Autumn Walnut Vinaigrette (below)
- Salt and freshly ground black pepper, to taste

1. Heat a cast-iron skillet and dry-toast the walnuts. Set aside.
2. Split the pitas with a fork or knife. Using a hot griddle or cast-iron skillet, grill the pitas for 1 or 2 minutes on each side.
3. Mix the walnuts, peppers, feta, and marjoram in a small bowl.
4. Line pitas with greens and cucumber slices. Stuff with pepper mixture. Drizzle with a generous amount of Autumn Walnut Vinaigrette. Season with salt and pepper to taste.

Autumn Walnut Vinaigrette
Makes about ½ cup

Mild and nutty flavored, this salad dressing is delicious with delicate mixed greens, such as mesclun. Autumn Walnut Vinaigrette also makes an excellent marinade for Rosemary-Roasted Peppers (page 47).

½ cup walnut oil
2 teaspoons lemon juice
1–2 tablespoons herb vinegar
Salt and freshly ground black pepper

Combine all ingredients, and whisk or stir to mix well. Refrigerate.

End-of-the-Garden Pasta Toss
Serves 4

If you had time to salvage some tomatoes and basil before Jack Frost ripped through the garden, here's a fragrant toast to the end of summer, perfect for a quick supper or weekend lunch. Serve with fresh bread for a complete meal.

1 tablespoon olive oil
2–4 cloves garlic, minced
2 cups coarsely chopped arugula
2–3 tomatoes, peeled and diced
1 pound linguine
4 ounces goat cheese, crumbled
2 tablespoons fresh marjoram
Salt and freshly ground black pepper, to taste
2 tablespoons coarsely chopped walnuts, dry-toasted

Rosemary-Roasted Peppers

Line a baking sheet with aluminum foil and spray with nonstick cooking spray. Cover the sheet with sprigs of rosemary. Select a colorful mixture of peppers, including hot peppers if desired. Cut bell types lengthwise into quarters, and arrange over rosemary. Place baking sheet directly under broiler. Check at 3 minutes, turn peppers, and broil 3 minutes more, or until they are evenly charred. Place peppers and rosemary in a paper bag and close. Let sit for 10 minutes; the steam makes skins easier to peel. Once peppers are cool, skin and seed them. Use immediately, or refrigerate for up to a week. Or, cut peppers into pieces, crumble some of the rosemary, and marinate all in Autumn Walnut Vinaigrette. Refrigerate for up to 10 days.

1. Heat the oil in a skillet over medium-low heat. Add the garlic and sauté for 1 or 2 minutes. Turn off heat. Stir in the arugula and the tomatoes. Cover to keep warm until the pasta is done.
2. Cook pasta according to package directions. Drain, reserving ¼ cup of cooking water, then place in a large serving bowl. Toss with vegetables, goat cheese, and marjoram. Add a little cooking water to blend ingredients well. Season with salt and pepper. Garnish with toasted walnuts. Serve hot.

Corn and Zucchini Fritters

Serves 4

These delicate patties are easy to prepare, and they make a wonderful supper or Sunday brunch. The supper version is great with sausage, cooked apples, and hot maple syrup. For an elegant brunch, serve with lox and sour cream (or yogurt) mixed with a little horseradish and garnished with minced chives.

2 small zucchini	1 teaspoon dried savory
1 teaspoon salt	⅛ teaspoon cayenne pepper
1 cup buttermilk	2 teaspoons baking soda
1 large egg	½ teaspoon baking powder
½ cup corn kernels, fresh or frozen	1 cup yellow cornmeal
½ teaspoon salt	Canola or peanut oil, for frying

1. Grate the zucchini and place in a large sieve set over a bowl. Sprinkle with 1 teaspoon salt. Let stand for 10 minutes, then squeeze out as much excess liquid as possible.
2. Beat the buttermilk with the egg in a medium bowl. Stir in the corn and zucchini.
3. Combine the dry ingredients in a larger bowl and mix well. Pour the zucchini mixture into the dry ingredients. Mix until just combined.
4. Heat the oil in a skillet. Fry fritters 2 to 3 minutes on one side, then flip and fry a minute or two longer, or until crispy and golden. Serve immediately.

Fennel and Rosemary-Roasted Chicken
Serves 4

Prepare the marinade Saturday morning and you'll be ready for easy entertaining that night. I usually bake the chicken in a Dutch oven with quartered carrots and potatoes, but this recipe also works well on the grill.

For the Marinade
- 3 tablespoons lemon juice
- ¼ cup tamari or soy sauce
- 3 tablespoons olive oil
- 6 cloves garlic, finely minced
- 4 chicken breasts, boneless and skinless

For the Herb Rub
- 1 teaspoon kosher salt
- 1 teaspoon black peppercorns
- 1 teaspoon crumbled, dried lemon verbena
- Pinch of cayenne pepper
- 1 tablespoon dried rosemary
- 1 tablespoon fennel seeds
- Several rosemary sprigs

1. Combine the lemon juice, tamari or soy sauce, oil, and garlic in a small bowl. Whisk well to blend.
2. Place the chicken in a large bowl. Pour the marinade over the chicken, and turn the pieces to coat. Cover and refrigerate for at least 2 hours. Turn several times to marinate evenly.
3. Preheat the oven to 425°F.
4. Grind the salt, peppercorns, lemon verbena, cayenne, rosemary, and fennel seeds in a food processor or with a mortar and pestle.
5. Remove the chicken from the marinade, shaking off any excess liquid. (Discard the marinade.) Place the chicken pieces in a roasting pan and sprinkle with the seasoning mix. Tuck the rosemary sprigs under the chicken pieces.
6. Cover the roasting pan and bake 20 to 25 minutes, or until chicken juices run clear.

Fennel

Delicious Seasonal Herbal Recipes

Baked Fish with Zested Parsley

SERVES 4

This simple recipe never fails. Coating the fish with yogurt keeps it moist without adding unnecessary fat. A little liquid added to the baking pan steams the fish, which also helps to keep it moist.

> 2 pounds flounder, halibut, cod, or other white fish
> 2 tablespoons plain, nonfat yogurt
> Zest from 1 lemon
> ½ cup chopped fresh flat-leaf parsley leaves
> 1 tablespoon minced fresh chervil
> 1 tablespoon minced fresh lemon thyme
> 2 cloves garlic, finely minced
> ½ teaspoon salt
> Pinch of cayenne pepper
> ½ cup unsweetened apple or white grape juice

1. Preheat the oven to 400°F.
2. Spray a 9 x 13-inch ovenproof baking dish with cooking spray. Place the fish in the baking dish and coat with the yogurt.
3. Blend the lemon zest, parsley, chervil, lemon thyme, garlic, salt, and cayenne in a small bowl. Sprinkle over the fish. Pour the fruit juice around the fish. Cover the dish with foil.
4. Bake for 20 minutes, or until fish flakes.

Herbed Yogurt Cheese

Here's another use for yogurt. Line a sieve with a double layer of coffee filters, and place it over a bowl. Put 2 cups of nonfat plain yogurt in the sieve. Cover with plastic wrap, and let drain at room temperature for 24 to 36 hours. Mix the resulting cheese with 1 teaspoon dry vegetable broth mix, 1 to 2 finely minced shallots, 1 tablespoon minced fresh parsley, 2 teaspoons minced fresh marjoram, and salt and pepper. A great spread for bagels!

Marinated Turkey Breast
Serves 4–6

For a small Thanksgiving dinner, roast a turkey breast. It tastes delicious and makes great leftovers for sandwiches. When ready to cook, fire up the grill if the weather permits, or place the meat in a roasting bag and bake. Rosemary honey (see page 18) is terrific in this recipe.

- 3- to 5-pound turkey breast
- 1 cup tamari or soy sauce
- ½ cup lemon juice
- ¼ cup honey
- ¼ cup peanut or sunflower oil
- 1 tablespoon toasted sesame oil
- 2 tablespoons Poultry Seasoning (page 10)
- Handful of rosemary sprigs

1. Place the turkey breast in a large self-sealing or heavy-duty plastic bag, and set the bagged turkey in a pan or bowl to avoid leakage.
2. Mix the tamari or soy sauce, lemon juice, honey, and oils in a small bowl. Pour this mixture into the bag, over the turkey. Marinate 8 to 12 hours, turning the bag occasionally to distribute the marinade.
3. Remove the turkey from the marinade. Discard any leftover marinade.
4. Sprinkle the turkey generously with Poultry Seasoning. If grilling, stuff rosemary sprigs under the skin of the turkey, trying not to split the skin. If using a roasting bag, place the rosemary in the bag along with the turkey.
5. Preheat the oven to 350°F. For oven roasting, cook turkey about 20 minutes per pound, or until the internal temperature at the thickest part of the breast registers 180°F on a meat thermometer. Let stand in the roasting bag for 10 minutes before removing. For grilling, roast 10 to 15 minutes on each side, then place cover on grill and cook about 20 to 30 minutes longer.

Cinnamon Basil Applesauce Cake

MAKES ONE 10-INCH TUBE CAKE

One of my favorite cakes, this herbed applesauce cake can be glazed or not. Instead of cinnamon basil, try lemon verbena or lemon balm for a different, but equally delicious, taste.

For the Cake
- 4 cups peeled and sliced tart apples
- 6 sprigs (2 inches each) cinnamon basil
- 2 cups currants
- 3½ cups unbleached flour
- 1½ cups sugar
- 2 teaspoons ground cinnamon
- 1 teaspoon ground ginger
- 1 teaspoon ground cloves
- ½ cup chopped black walnuts
- ¾ cup vegetable shortening
- 4 teaspoons baking soda, dissolved in 1 cup lukewarm water

For the Cinnamon Basil Icing
- ½ cup packed cinnamon basil leaves
- ¼ cup boiling water
- 1 tablespoon softened unsalted butter
- 1½ cups confectioners' sugar
- 1 teaspoon lemon zest

1. Preheat the oven to 350°F. Grease a 10-inch tube pan.
2. Place the apples in a large saucepan. Cover and cook gently until apples are soft. Remove from heat, add the cinnamon basil sprigs, cover, and let sit for 20 minutes. Remove the cinnamon basil.
3. Whip the apples briskly with a whisk to make a coarse applesauce. Stir in the currants. Cover the pan again to keep warm.
4. Mix flour, sugar, spices, and nuts in a large bowl. Add shortening to the hot applesauce, and stir until it melts. Add the baking soda water to the applesauce. Pour the applesauce mixture into the flour mixture. Mix until well blended. Pour into the prepared pan.
5. Bake 1¼ hours, or until a toothpick inserted in the cake comes out clean. Remove it from the pan and cool.
6. For the icing, in a small saucepan, steep the cinnamon basil leaves in the boiling water for 20 minutes. Remove the leaves and simmer the infusion for a few minutes to reduce the liquid by half. Let cool.
7. Beat the butter, sugar, and lemon zest. Add enough cinnamon basil infusion to make a thin glaze. Pour it over the cooled cake.

Winter Recipes

The solstice marks the beginning of winter in my part of the world. After the celebratory flurry of holiday visiting and rich treats, it feels good to sit back and stir a simple pot of bean soup.

I enjoy the quietness of winter more each passing year. With not as much to do, I'm more content to be, well, a human being rather than a human doing. Cooking is a more relaxed affair, as the kitchen heat and penetrating fragrances of rosemary, bay, and thyme invite me to linger and then to call a friend to share scones and Rosemary-Goldenrod Jelly (page 18) with herbal tea. This is a good time to inventory the pantry and freezer, and dig into the winter stash with less caution.

Texas Caviar

Serves 8

Black-eyed peas are traditional southern fare for New Year's Day. Serve with tortilla chips or grilled pitas.

- 1½ cups dried black-eyed peas
- 1 sprig (3 inches) sage
- 1 dried chipotle chili
- 3 cups boiling water
- 4 scallions, minced (use some of the green)
- 2–3 roasted jalapeño peppers, peeled, seeded, and chopped
- ⅓ cup walnut or peanut oil
- ¼ cup apple cider or herb vinegar
- ¼ cup lime juice
- Salt and freshly ground black pepper, to taste
- ⅓ cup packed, minced fresh cilantro

1. Wash the peas, discarding any that are imperfect. Place the peas in a 3-quart saucepan with the sage and chili. Stir in the boiling water. Return to a boil, cover, and adjust heat to a gentle simmer. Cook for 35 to 45 minutes, or until peas are tender but not mushy.
2. Whisk the remaining ingredients in a small bowl. Pour over peas, and stir until well combined; then pour into a bowl and cover.
3. Marinate peas in the refrigerator at least overnight — three days is better. Serve chilled or at room temperature.

Delicious Seasonal Herbal Recipes

Rosemary Chickpea Appetizer Bake
Serves 4–6

What a wonderful, finger-licking dish to share with good friends! Mix the batter early in the day so you can pop it in the oven when guests arrive. Serve as soon as it's cool enough to handle, by breaking it apart and eating it with your fingers.

- 1½ cups water
- 1 cup chickpea flour
- 4 tablespoons olive oil
- ½ teaspoon salt
- 1 tablespoon chopped fresh rosemary
- Lots of freshly ground black pepper

1. Pour the water into a medium-size bowl. Whisk in the chickpea flour until lumps disappear. Let sit for 3 to 4 hours.
2. Preheat oven to 500°F. Pour the oil into an 11 × 15-inch metal baking pan. Turn pan to coat bottom.
3. Whisk the salt and rosemary into the chickpea flour mixture. Spread the mixture evenly in the pan. It should be no more than ¼ inch thick. Bake 20 minutes.
4. Remove the pan from the oven and sprinkle with the freshly ground pepper while it's still hot. May be stored for several weeks in the refrigerator.

Herbal Christmas Tree

Wrap an upside-down, circular tomato cage with grapevines, string white lights, and festoon with fragrant branches of rosemary or sage. You can add natural ornaments such as mini-grapevine wreaths decorated with dried garlic chive flower heads and wild rose hips; potpourri-covered balls; and tiny tussie-mussies wrapped in lamb's ears leaves for doilies.

Roasted Squash Butter

MAKES ABOUT 3 CUPS

Delicious served as a dip with crisp celery sticks or garlic toast, squash butter also makes a satisfying low-calorie spread for muffins and other breads. Store, refrigerated, for at least a week. You can also make this recipe using sweet potatoes or carrots.

- 3–4 sprigs fresh sage
- 1 medium butternut squash
- 1 small onion, finely minced
- 2 cloves garlic, finely minced
- 1 tablespoon olive oil
- ½ teaspoon dried marjoram
- 2 tablespoons tahini
- 3 tablespoons barley miso (available at natural-food stores)

1. Preheat oven to 425°F.
2. Line a roasting pan with aluminum foil and spray with nonstick cooking spray. Lay the sage sprigs in the pan.
3. Cut the squash in half lengthwise. Clean out the seeds. Place the squash cut-sides down over the sage leaves. Bake 45 minutes, or until the squash is soft to the touch. Cool.
4. Sauté the onion and garlic in the oil over medium heat until they turn light brown. Reserve.
5. Remove the flesh from the squash and place it in a food processor with the cooked onion and garlic and the remaining ingredients. Process until smooth. This dip is best served at room temperature.

Caramelized Onion Sauce

MAKES 3–4 CUPS

Fragrant onions and thyme, cooked until sweetly savory, are delicious as a spread on chewy herbed breads. For a special treat, grill Swiss cheese on pumpernickel bread, cut into wedges, and let guests slather the onion sauce on top. You can also toss it with pasta, spread it on pizza, or use it as a sauce for grilled fish or meats. It's even great on a simple cheese omelet. Use the heaviest skillet in the house to help prevent the onions from scorching.

Delicious Seasonal Herbal Recipes

3 tablespoons olive oil	1 cup apple cider
5 large Spanish onions, thinly sliced	1 teaspoon balsamic vinegar
	¼ cup fresh, finely minced thyme
6–8 cloves garlic, finely minced	Salt and pepper, to taste

1. Heat the olive oil in a heavy skillet over medium heat. Add the onions and garlic. (If your skillet is small, you can add the onions in small amounts, continuing to add more as they cook down.) Lower heat to a gentle simmer and stir. Cook, uncovered, until the onions are golden in color and greatly reduced in volume — about 1 hour. Stir frequently to prevent scorching.
2. Add the cider, vinegar, and thyme, and cook until the liquid has been absorbed. Season to taste with the salt and pepper.

Warm Salad of Leeks and Collards with Tahini

Serves 4–6

I like this savory twist on cooked greens any time of day: for breakfast with toast or as a side dish with dinner.

1 large bunch collards, julienned, 5–6 cups	3 tablespoons Opal Basil-Garlic-Black Peppercorn Vinegar (page 118)
1 tablespoon olive oil	⅓ cup tahini
6–8 cloves garlic, finely minced	1 tablespoon tamari or soy sauce
2 large leeks, white part cut into thin rounds	¼ cup minced garlic chives

1. Bring an 8-quart stockpot of water to a boil.
2. Clean the collards and remove the tough inner rib. Roll the leaves lengthwise and cut them crosswise into thin strips.
3. Cook the greens in boiling water for 3 to 4 minutes, until almost tender. Drain them in a colander, and run cold water over them to cool. Reserve.
4. Heat the oil in a large skillet over medium-low heat. Sauté the garlic and leeks until they begin to soften. Stir in the collards, add the vinegar, tahini, and tamari or soy sauce, and sauté until collards are heated through. Stir in the garlic chives. Serve warm.

Winter Substitute for Chives

In central Maryland, I can scavenge garlic mustard *(Alliaria officinalis)* from the woods' edge all winter. If this plant grows in your area, cut a handful of the round leaves, remove the stems, and chop the leaves finely. Use it as you would chives, raw or lightly cooked, to add a mild garlic flavor to soups, salads, herb butter, softened cheeses, and other savories.

Classy White-Bean Soup
Serves 8

Dressed up with Garlic Butter Drizzle, and served with salad and good bread, this simple soup is ready for company. I generally use Great Northern beans or navy beans; cannellini beans are good, too. If you have a pressure cooker, the beans will be ready to puree in less than 1 hour. For a different twist, substitute last summer's frozen pesto, thawed and warmed, for the Garlic Butter Drizzle.

- 2 cups dried white beans
- 3 tablespoons olive oil
- 2 medium onions, chopped
- 2 shallots, finely minced
- 6 cups water or vegetable stock
- 2 bay leaves
- 3 sprigs (6 inches) fresh thyme
- 1 teaspoon dried savory
- Salt and freshly ground black pepper, to taste
- Fresh parsley, finely chopped, for garnish

For the Garlic Butter Drizzle

- 2 tablespoons olive oil
- 1 tablespoon unsalted butter
- 4 cloves garlic, finely minced

1. Soak the beans in water overnight. Drain and wash them until the water runs clear. Reserve.
2. Heat the oil in a large saucepan. Sauté the onions and shallots over medium-low heat until they begin to soften. Add the beans, water or stock, and bay leaves. Cook 2 to 3 hours, or until the beans are tender.

3. Stir in the thyme and savory. Cover the pan and let sit until it cools slightly (at least 15 minutes).
4. Remove the bay leaves and thyme sprigs. Puree the soup.
5. To make the Garlic Butter Drizzle, heat the oil and butter in a small skillet over medium heat. Sauté the garlic until it begins to turn golden brown. Remove from the heat.
6. Ladle the soup into bowls, add a little Garlic Butter Drizzle, and garnish with the parsley and salt and pepper to taste.

Roasted Herbed Cauliflower
Serves 4–6

Serving the cauliflower whole creates an impressive dish that's deceptively simple to prepare. A large covered casserole dish or Dutch oven works best for roasting. Line the bottom with aluminum foil or parchment paper, as the honey may stick to the bottom of the pan. Alternatively, use a purchased roasting bag. Rosemary herb honey (see page 18) is excellent for this dish.

1 perfect head of cauliflower
½ cup herb honey
1 teaspoon ground coriander seed
2 tablespoons grated fresh gingerroot
1 tablespoon herb vinegar
2 fresh bay leaves, torn into several pieces
1 teaspoon roasted sesame oil
½ teaspoon salt
1 teaspoon freshly ground black pepper
5–6 sprigs fresh rosemary or thyme
1 cup water

Bay

1. Preheat oven to 400°F.
2. Remove any greens from the cauliflower.
3. Mix the remaining ingredients, except the rosemary and water, in a small bowl to make the dressing.
4. Place the rosemary in the bottom of the lined roasting pan. Place

the cauliflower in the pan, leafy-side down. Drizzle the head with the dressing. Pour the water into the bottom of the pan. Bake, covered, for 30 minutes.
5. Remove the pan from the oven to baste. Add more water if needed. Bake 20 minutes more, or until tender. Baste again.
6. Serve hot or at room temperature.

Broiled Onions and Portobello Mushrooms
Serves 4

We enjoy this rich-tasting but low-calorie side dish with turkey burgers. It also makes a nice topping for pizza. Any leftovers are a fine addition to grilled cheese sandwiches or omelets.

- 1 large onion, thinly sliced
- 1–2 portobello mushrooms, thinly sliced
- 1–2 tablespoons olive oil
- 1–2 tablespoons tamari or soy sauce
- 1 tablespoon minced fresh thyme

1. Line a baking sheet with aluminum foil. Spread the onions and mushrooms over the foil. Drizzle with a little olive oil and tamari or soy sauce. Mix the vegetables around to coat evenly. Let sit for an hour. Sprinkle with the thyme.
2. Broil the marinated onions and mushrooms about 6 to 8 minutes. Turn the vegetables midway to ensure even browning. Serve hot.

Sagey Turkey Burgers
Serves 4

These turkey burgers are the best! Ricotta cheese gives the turkey a smoother texture and miso deepens the flavor. Bake in a loaf if you prefer. We like turkey burgers with Broiled Onions and Portobello Mushrooms. If you're really hungry, open a jar of tomatoes and simmer them with a little dill or basil pesto as another side dish.

- 1 pound ground turkey
- 2 cups cooked rice
- ½ cup ricotta cheese
- 2 tablespoons dark barley miso
- ½ cup finely minced fresh sage
- Freshly ground black pepper, to taste

Delicious Seasonal Herbal Recipes

1. Combine all the ingredients in a mixing bowl. Shape into patties.
2. Spray the skillet with nonstick cooking spray. Fry the turkey burgers over medium heat, turning once, until done, about 8 to 10 minutes total. Serve hot on a toasted bun.

Sweet-and-Sour Glazed Chicken

Serves 4

This is a nice change from plain roasted chicken. It's extra good served with basmati rice, sautéed spinach, and corn bread. Slide a few fat carrots or sweet potatoes into the roasting pan if you like.

- Several large sprigs fresh rosemary or sage
- 1 chicken (3–5 pounds), cut into pieces
- 1 cup orange marmalade spiked with 1 teaspoon dried tarragon
- 4–6 cloves garlic, finely minced
- 1 tablespoon tamari or soy sauce
- Paprika
- Salt, to taste

1. Preheat oven to 400°F. Place the rosemary in the bottom of a Dutch oven. Lay the chicken pieces on the herbs.
2. Mix the marmalade, garlic, and tamari or soy sauce in a small bowl. Pour the dressing over the chicken and turn to coat. Sprinkle the chicken with paprika and salt.
3. Cover and bake 25 to 30 minutes, or until juices run clear. The internal temperature of the chicken should be 190°F.

Sage

Herbed Tamari Nuts

Makes 1 pound

Use any combination of nuts that you like to make this delicious snack. My favorite is almonds and sunflower seeds, which I mix with raisins when serving. If you include seeds like sunflower or pumpkin in the mix, coat them separately and add to the baking tray about 30 minutes into the cooking, as they take less time to roast.

1 large egg white
1 tablespoon herb honey
1 tablespoon tamari or soy sauce
¼ cup minced fresh rosemary or sage
1 pound nuts or seeds, raw and shelled

1. Preheat oven to 250°F.
2. Beat the egg white until frothy. Whisk in the honey, tamari or soy sauce, and herbs.
3. Pour the dressing over the nuts in a small bowl. Stir until the nuts are well coated. Spread in a single layer on a nonstick baking sheet or on a regular sheet lined with parchment paper.
4. Bake 1 hour, turning several times. Cool. Store in airtight tins.

Southwestern-Style Spoonbread

SERVES 6

Eggs and cheese and butter — mmm. This spoonbread isn't low in calories, but it's very good. If you don't have any marinated jalapeños, use canned green chilis. Use more or less cayenne, depending on how hot you like things.

1 cup cornmeal
1 teaspoon baking soda
1 teaspoon dried marjoram
2 eggs
⅔ cup buttermilk
3 tablespoons unsalted butter, melted
1 can (15 ounces) creamed corn
⅛ teaspoon cayenne pepper

For the Filling
1 cup shredded Monterey Jack cheese
⅓ cup marinated jalapeños (see page 47), or canned peppers

1. Preheat oven to 400°F. Butter a soufflé dish.
2. Mix the cornmeal, baking soda, and marjoram in a medium-size bowl.
3. Beat the eggs, buttermilk, and melted butter in another bowl. Add the creamed corn and cayenne pepper, and stir until well combined. Beat the cornmeal mixture into the egg mixture, stirring only until combined.
4. Pour half the batter into the baking dish. Sprinkle batter with the cheese and marinated jalapeños. Cover with the remaining batter.
5. Bake for 35 to 40 minutes, or until set.

Chai

MAKES 4 CUPS

Chai is a fragrant, Indian-style tea. Holy basil is the secret ingredient in this recipe, but any basil is good in chai. For best results, use a strong black tea such as Assam or Darjeeling.

- 1 cup milk (either low-fat or soy)
- 3 cups water
- 3 cardamom pods, coarsely crushed
- 3–4 whole cloves
- 1 cinnamon stick (1 inch)
- 1–3 black peppercorns, coarsely crushed
- 3–4 teaspoons loose black tea
- 4–6 sprigs holy basil (or 1 frozen cube, see page 151)
- Freshly grated nutmeg, for garnish

Heat milk, water, cardamom, cloves, cinnamon sticks, and peppercorns in a saucepan over medium heat. When mixture is just ready to boil, remove from heat; add tea and holy basil. Cover and let sit 5 minutes. Strain, and serve topped with the grated nutmeg.

Pine-Needle Tea

After the garden is blackened by frost and you're longing for something freshly picked, gather fragrant pine needles for afternoon tea. A handful (24 to 30 needles) is all you need. Bring 4 cups of water to a boil, and pour over the snipped pine needles. Cover the pot and steep 5 to 10 minutes. Strain and serve the mildly resinous tea warm, with honey and lemon if desired. Believe it or not, pine needles have a significant amount of vitamin C!

Safety first: Do not use the needles from your Christmas tree if purchased or soaked in preservative-treated water. Preservatives sprayed on Christmas trees and added to the water in the tree stand are extremely toxic. Take special care to protect young children and pets from this hazard, as well.

CHAPTER 3

BEGINNER'S GUIDE TO HERBAL
Housekeeping

Too busy to clean? Herbal housekeeping can actually save you time, as well as money, while providing you with safe products that solve all kinds of household problems. Most of my cleaning formulas are simple to make and can be prepared in advance to be stored, conveniently ready for use as needed. With them, you can make your home a sweet-smelling haven for you and your family.

Cleaning with herbs is not only easy and effective, but it's also good for our earth. With the information and formulas in this book, you will soon be an expert at using herbs to clean just about anything, even if you've never used herbs in this way before.

Benefits of Herbal Housekeeping

Like me, you may find the repetitiveness of housecleaning boring. But I feel calmer when my house is clean, and I am better able to cope with the demands of my life when it is tidy, sensibly organized, and beautiful. To help make everyday chores more enjoyable, I've researched and experimented for more than 25 years, finding new ways to use the aromatic herbs and essential oils I love. My "cleaning team" is Rose, Melissa, Rosemary, Basil, and other herbs, whose scents sweeten my tasks.

What is less evident, but perhaps more important, is that the same herbs that provide sensory pleasure also combat all kinds of nasty microorganisms lurking about on the surfaces and in the air of our homes. Hyssop, mints, lavender, roses, lemon balm, sage, thyme — all of these herbs and many others have been used for centuries to clean and freshen.

HERBAL TRADITIONS

As John Parkinson wrote in 1629, "Many herbs and flowers with their fragrant smells do comfort, and as it were revive the spirits and perfume the whole house." Long before supermarkets and modern manufacturers of cleaning products existed, people got by with what they could grow, make, or trade. Nine out of ten of them were

Soapy Waters

Commercial soap did not become widely available until the early 19th century. So what did people clean with before that? Plant ashes were used to make lye, urine was aged for its ammonia content, and, if they could afford it, women used vinegar. Small wonder that herbs were appreciated for their fragrance and use in "sweete washing waters"!

employed in agricultural pursuits and thus were likely to recognize an herb that grew in the meadow, hedgerow, or woods, and to know a good bit about its uses.

In the Middle Ages, when most cottages had floors of pounded earth, householders brought fresh plant material indoors to strew around, providing a pleasant softness underfoot and perfuming the dark and smoky interior. The plants served to keep insect populations somewhat under control, too. Wealthy people carried pomanders of ambergris, musk, orange, and spices, or wore them around their necks or waists to protect against disease.

CREATING A NEW TRADITION

Like my ancestors, I like natural materials. And as you will see, many herbs have qualities that can help you clean, disinfect, scent your home, and deter pests. Plus, you can enhance the power of these herbs by blending materials like vinegar, alcohol, minerals, and essential oils with them.

Vinegar. One of the most natural partners for herbs is vinegar, because its acidity makes it a natural disinfectant: Bacteria prefer a more alkaline environment.

Supplies and Methods

The methods I use are so simple that everyone can make their own cleaning products. Most of the time, you will be adding herbs — either fresh or dried, and sometimes a combination of the two — to a solvent, such as water, vinegar, alcohol, glycerin, ammonia, or oil. The basic formulas are on pages 78–84.

Most of the materials I use to make my herbal home products can be readily purchased at your local pharmacy, or grocery, hardware, paint, or health food store. For bulk purchases of herbs and other natural products, check Herbal Resources, starting on page 152, for mail-order suppliers.

Other solutions. You can also extract herbs in water, glycerin, or alcohols of various sorts: grain, isopropyl, or denatured grain. Occasionally, herbs are infused directly in oils. Adding 3 percent essential oil to a fixed oil is an easier, faster, but more expensive, way to achieve an effect similar to that of an infused oil without all the work. The solution you choose depends on the end use of the product.

Minerals. Herbs can also be combined with minerals, like baking soda, washing soda, salt, various clays, chalk, and others to do their work. I like to use them with natural soaps, including Murphy's Oil Soap, which is made from pine bark; Dr. Bronner's Liquid Castile Soaps; and, occasionally, grated bar soaps.

Essential oils. Essential oils concentrate the cleaning and disinfecting powers of plants. I blend purchased oils with liquid soaps, then add them to solutions they are soluble in: glycerin, alcohol, or oil. Of course, I also use them in potpourri and evaporate them in diffusers. Their intense fragrances can be overpowering, but when they are used properly they add a wonderful, welcoming ambiance. I consider the use of essential oils aromatherapy for my home, but everyone in the house benefits from their fragrant ability to raise the spirits while they disinfect.

Caution: Chemicals at Work

Today, the average home in the United States contains more chemicals than were found in a typical 19th-century chemistry lab. In fact, estimates project that every home uses 25 gallons of hazardous chemicals each year, and has from 50 to 100 pounds of dangerous materials requiring professional hazardous-waste disposal sitting around the kitchen, bathroom, basement, and garage. At the same time, 15 percent of the U.S. population is sensitive to chemicals in common household products, and evidence is mounting that this witches' brew of chemicals in our environment is responsible for chronic, long-term health effects of a serious nature for many more of us.

Essential Supplies

You may already have everything you need in your kitchen to make herbal cleaning supplies. If not, you can probably improvise some items and purchase others. Depending upon which types of formulas you intend to make and use, you may not need everything described here.

The equipment used to process herbal formulas should be made of glass, heat-treated glass, glass-ceramic fusions (such as Corningware), ceramic (nonleaded glazes), enameled steel, enameled cast iron, or stainless steel. These materials are less reactive and will not alter the qualities of the herbs, interfere with chemical reactions, or be damaged by the corrosive nature of some essential oils or vinegar the way plastic, aluminum, cast iron, and other metals might be.

CLEANING

A colander and a salad spinner are handy for washing any fresh herbs that need to be cleaned. You may have to clean roots with a stiff vegetable brush, or if the skin is particularly tough, with a vegetable parer.

GRINDING

A mortar and pestle are useful for bruising seeds or grinding small quantities of herbs. A small electric coffee grinder works well, but use it solely for herbs. Pulverize dried herbs by rubbing them between your hands, or place large quantities in a pillowcase or locking plastic bag, and roll over them with a rolling pin until they're crushed.

CUTTING, CHOPPING, AND GRATING

I often use a sharp knife and a hardwood cutting board that I reserve only for herb chopping. You can also use scissors to cut up some herbs, or a food processor to mince herbs and to grate roots. For small quantities, you can use a standard, four-sided hand grater.

Wood vs. Plastic

Microbiologists at the University of Wisconsin Food Research Institute at Madison discovered that wood cutting boards are naturally better than plastic ones. Plastic encourages bacterial growth, while the porous nature of the wood pulls moisture from microorganisms, causing their rapid death. Although plastics are now made with antibiotics added, experts feel they contribute to the alarming speed with which microorganisms are becoming immune to antibiotics. To prevent bacterial contamination, wash all cutting boards in hot soapy water after each use. Rinse. Sprinkle with baking soda, then spray with herbal vinegar. Let stand 10 minutes. Rinse again, and dry thoroughly.

MEASURING

It's helpful to have a selection of glass and stainless-steel measuring cups and spoons in different sizes. If you intend to do a lot of work with essential oils, you may want to get a milliliter measure, or several glass eyedroppers. A scale that can weigh in ounces and grams is essential for some formulas.

Safety first. Always wear gloves when weighing or measuring potentially irritating or sensitizing ingredients like essentials oils, borax, washing soda, and ammonia.

Electronic scale, measuring tools, and rubber gloves

MIXING

Sometimes a blender is useful for mixing liquids, but powders and dry ingredients should be mixed in a bowl. A selection of Pyrex or Corelle bowls of various sizes may be the most useful items in my

Household Herbs

kitchen. For large quantities, I've been known to use my biggest stainless-steel pot. Depending upon the size of the batch, you may need to use various-sized stainless-steel utensils, from teaspoons to serving spoons.

Safety first. *When working with powdered ingredients, wear a dust mask to protect mucous membranes. Masks are inexpensive, and readily available at hardware and paint stores.*

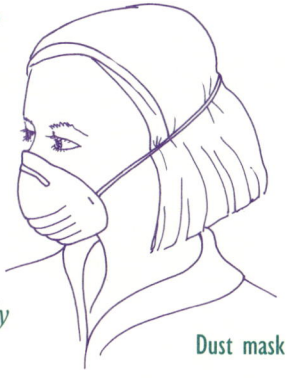

Dust mask

HEATING

I use a whistling stainless-steel teakettle to heat water, but an enameled one would be okay, too. Thermometers are essential if you're making formulas for wood and leather moisturizing and polishing creams. Double boilers are needed for formulas that use wax.

Teakettle and thermometers

AGING

Some formulas, and most herbal extractions (except infusions, page 78, and decoctions, page 79), require a steeping or aging period. This is done in wide-mouthed glass jars with sealing lids. I keep several dozen pint, quart, half-gallon, and gallon jars for this purpose.

STRAINING

Herbal extractions should be strained before use. I usually just pour small batches through a stainless-steel tea strainer. Large batches go in a yogurt strainer, made of fine-meshed fabric, placed inside a glass measuring cup. Some herbalists strain through layers of muslin, either suspended like a jelly bag or tied over a bowl.

Straining separates most of the solids from the liquid.

Beginner's Guide to Herbal Housekeeping

Perfectionists will want to filter the strained liquid, using an unbleached or oxygen-bleached coffee filter. I almost always skip this step for household formulas. I think it's just extra work, but if you strain through a coarse strainer, you may need to filter.

Straining equipment

STORING

I use stainless-steel funnels to transfer mixtures to storage containers: a narrow-tipped one for liquids and a wide-mouthed canning funnel for powdered and dry blends. I store liquids in various-sized amber glass bottles. The color blocks light that would degrade the contents. I use wide-mouthed glass pint jars for waxes and polishes. Powdered formulas can be kept in wide-mouthed jars or tins with a tight seal but should be put in small shaker jars, such as Parmesan cheese containers, for use.

Funnel and storage containers

LABELING

Once your herbal cleaning supplies are packaged, label and date them. Sometimes I run off labels on my laser printer, but a permanent marker or china pencil will work well, too. The important thing is to make sure no one uses floor polish as a medicinal ointment, or drinks toilet cleaner thinking it's an herbal elixir.

MISCELLANEOUS EQUIPMENT

A few more items come in handy, such as candy molds, mini-muffin pans, or butter or cookie molds for casting beeswax. I've made a hobby over the years of collecting kitchen items from estate sales, outlet stores, and catalogs.

Basic Ingredients

Many herbal cleaning formulas are based on a few simple techniques, which you'll learn about later in this chapter. But before I show you how to proceed with techniques, you need a bit of information about some common ingredients that you'll use over and over again when you begin to make your own housekeeping products: alcohol, ammonia, essential oils, fixatives, fixed oils, glycerin, vinegar, and, most basic of all, water. Many other ingredients appear in the recipes, and on page 120 you'll find a chart, Herbal Housekeeping Ingredients, that describes each one, and tells you its uses and where to get it.

Alcohol. Alcohol is a clear, colorless, volatile, flammable liquid. Both essential oils and water mix with alcohol, making alcohol a necessity for formulas requiring the cleaning power or fragrance of essential oils, since essential oils don't mix with water. You can also use alcohol to extract chemicals from both fresh and dried herbs.

Grain alcohol, also called ethyl alcohol, is derived from yeast fermentation of grain and is sold at liquor stores. Ask for 190-proof alcohol, which is 95 percent alcohol. I feel it's the safest alcohol to use for household formulas.

Denatured alcohol is sold at paint stores for about a third of the price of grain alcohol. A poisonous substance is added to it to make it unfit for human consumption, but it is still suitable for other purposes.

Isopropyl alcohol is made from propylene. Commonly known as rubbing alcohol, it's sold at pharmacies. It is more toxic than grain alcohol and less toxic than denatured alcohol, but is sold for external use only. It costs about the same as denatured alcohol.

In my cleaning formulas, I specify a particular type of alcohol, and also whether any substitutions are allowable. Let your budget be your guide. Whatever type of alcohol you use, be sure to clearly label NOT INTENDED FOR HUMAN CONSUMPTION. Call a Poison Control Center immediately if you suspect that anyone has ingested household cleaning formulas containing nonpotable alcohol.

Label all homemade products.

Ammonia. A diluted solution of ammonium hydroxide, ammonia is a clear liquid with a pungent, penetrating odor. It has many cleaning and laundry applications because it is especially good at cutting grease and cleaning woolens. The fumes are unpleasant, and I clean with ammonia solutions only when I have a really heavy-duty cleaning chore and can ventilate the room by opening doors and windows.

Safety first. Never combine ammonia with bleach or a product containing bleach. A chemical reaction occurs that releases potentially toxic fumes. Cleaning formulas made with ammonia should be clearly labeled NOT INTENDED FOR HUMAN CONSUMPTION.

Essential oils. Essential oils are concentrated volatile compounds that are commercially steam-distilled or pressed from aromatic plant material. To understand how concentrated these oils are, note that herbs rarely contain more than 2 percent (and often less than 0.5 percent) of

Testing for Allergic Reactions

It's important to understand how to test for allergic reactions before getting into a cleaning solution up to your elbows. Always do a patch test for every new ingredient in any formula to which your skin will be exposed. Apply the substance as described below, cover with an adhesive bandage, then check in 24 hours. If your skin is raised, bumpy, red, raw, irritated, oozing, or otherwise damaged, do not use the ingredient, or wear gloves when working with it.

For liquid materials. To test strong herb tea infusions and decoctions and diluted soaps, or fixed oils like olive, almond, sesame, hazelnut, canola, and safflower, apply a few drops to the inside of your forearm.

For essential oils. Place 1 drop oil into a teaspoon of a fixed oil, such as olive, walnut, mineral, or jojoba, that you know is safe for use on your skin. Apply a little to the inside of your forearm.

For dry materials. If you're working with dry materials like powdered roses and arrowroot starch, dissolve them in a small amount of water (enough to make a paste), and apply to the inside of your forearm.

Storing Essential Oils

When essential oils age, oxidation occurs, rendering them more likely to cause skin sensitization and less capable of antibacterial activity and immune-system enhancement. In *Essential Oil Safety: A Guide for Health Professionals,* Robert Tisserand and Tony Balacs recommend that essential oils be stored in amber glass bottles and used within 6 months to 1 year of opening. Pine and citrus oils degrade the most quickly, as early as 6 months after the bottle is first opened. To double their life, store all oils in the refrigerator. Be sure that everyone in your household understands that they should not be ingested or handled undiluted. If you have young children, keep oils in a locked cupboard, drawer, or toolbox.

their essential oil. Oils can easily be mixed with alcohol, and in some cases, with glycerine. Oils that are solvent-extracted are called absolutes and may contain small amounts of the solvent used. Purchase essential oils and absolutes from a local health food store or mail-order supplier.

The chart on pages 124–25 lists 21 popular essential oils; following that is a chart that includes essential oils with fixative properties. Besides those, many other essential oils are good for personal and household aromatherapeutic uses: bergamot, black pepper, chamomile, geranium, hyssop, jasmine absolute, juniper berry, laurel leaf, lemon eucalyptus, myrrh, neroli (orange blossom), niaouli, petitgrain (orange leaf and twig), red thyme, rose absolute, sandalwood, vanilla oleoresin, white thyme, and ylang-ylang. Some are especially effective disinfectants. Thyme oil, for instance, contains thymol, which is more powerful than phenol, the chemical used to clean hospitals.

Safety first. *Never take essential oils internally.*

Fixatives can improve all the scented formulas in this book. These fragrant roots, seeds, and resins, as well as some animal-derived materials, possess the special ability to blend the other fragrances in a mixture into a new scent, then to release that scent in a slow, controlled man-

Florentine iris

ner. Violet-scented orrisroot, the dried, aged rhizome of Florentine iris, is a favorite of potpourri makers, but many other plants have fixative properties as well. Fixatives have interesting, sometimes strong, even peculiar scents of their own, along with their capacity to blend.

You can grow your own, or purchase dried botanicals, essential oils, or absolutes. Work them into every scented product you create, to make the fragrances linger longer, and to take the edge off harsh or disparate fragrances. You'll find a chart beginning on page 126 that lists 28 useful fixatives.

Fixed oils are nonvolatile vegetable or animal oils. I recommend linseed, olive, walnut, mineral, and jojoba oils. Find linseed oil at paint, hardware, and home center stores; purchase edible oils at health food and grocery stores or from a mail-order supplier.

Glycerin is a clear, odorless, sweet-tasting, viscous alcohol that is a by-product when animal or vegetable fats and oils are made into soap. It's useful for both extracting and preserving herbal products. Since essential oils mix with it, and it mixes with liquid soaps, it also serves as a vehicle for adding fragrance to manufactured soap products. You can buy glycerin at pharmacies, health food stores, and from mail-order suppliers.

Vinegar is a dilute acetic acid made by fermenting grains or fruits. When it has been distilled to remove the brown color, it's labeled as distilled white vinegar. It's available at grocery stores; stock up when it's on sale.

Water is wonderful stuff! The water used in these formulas should be filtered, if at all possible. If not, well water is preferable to distilled water. Get it from your tap or buy it at the grocery store. I use double-filtered tap water.

SIMPLE TECHNIQUES FOR HERBAL SOLUTIONS

Although I make many "simples" (the term for formulas that use only one herb), I most enjoy making compounds, which require multiple herbs. Not only do herbal compounds create unique fragrances, but they also allow you to use more than one herb to fight particular organisms like staph, strep, and herpes.

Using dried herbs makes it possible to combine plants that peak

Safety First Guidelines

- Pay attention to use restrictions and safety information in this book and on the containers of any raw ingredients incorporated into your cleaning products.

- Allergy-test any ingredients that your skin will be exposed to (see Testing for Allergic Reactions on page 72), and if you are prone to allergic reactions, test all ingredients before working with them.

- Always wear gloves when working with undiluted essential oils, strong soap solutions, minerals like washing soda, and chemicals like ammonia.

- If you spill undiluted essential oil on your skin, dilute it immediately with any fixed oil before attempting to wash it off.

- Always wear a dust mask when working with powdered ingredients.

- Always ensure adequate ventilation when working with essential oils, ammonia, and other strongly scented products.

- Never mix any product containing bleach with any product containing ammonia, as the combination produces noxious fumes.

- Label all cleaning products with a complete list of all ingredients and any cautions.

- Keep the local Poison Control Center phone number written in a handy place.

- Store all potentially dangerous ingredients and products in places that children and pets cannot get into, just as you would with any other cleaning supplies. A locked cupboard is best.

- Store any flammable products and ingredients, like waxes, alcohols, and solvents, in glass or metal containers away from heat and open flames.

- Carefully dispose of flammable rags impregnated with waxes or solvents.

- Keep a fire extinguisher (or a large box of baking soda) in your kitchen, garage, and basement.

at different times of the year, and purchasing herbs lets you use herbs that require different growing conditions than you can provide in your garden. But you can also let your herb garden guide your choice. Each week something new peaks in the garden, so I tend to go out,

Gather fresh herbs in a shallow basket.

basket in hand, to collect whatever is there. During the garden season, my formulas are composed of fresh herbs that are at their best at the same time.

USING HERB FORMULAS SAFELY

Many herbs and essential oils that are powerful antiseptic disinfectants or insect repellents have components that range from very mildly toxic to seriously toxic if they are ingested as a concentrated essential oil. But most — even those with dangerous components — are quite safe when used in extract form in cleaning solutions, or I wouldn't use them. I provide safety information wherever appropriate because I want to help you decide whether to use a particular herb or essential oil or to select another, safer one, even if the alternate choices might be less effective. For instance, if you are expecting a child, you should work only with the safest, least toxic materials. Formulations for cleaning a baby's room should be made with safe herbs like lavender, roses, chamomile, and spearmint, rather than the stronger wormwood, southernwood, tansy, and rue. For more safety tips, see page 75.

THE BASIC FORMULAS

The basic method for making an herbal extraction is simple: you combine finely chopped fresh or dried herb with a liquid. Making housekeeping recipes doesn't require the exactitude you might aim for when you're making an extraction for medicinal use. I make them using the folk method, which requires no weighing or measuring.

Everything goes much faster that way, and I achieve perfectly satisfactory results with the least amount of effort.

Mixing. I harvest fresh herbs, flowers, or other plant materials in the morning, then chop or cut the plant material with a knife or scissors. If you're using dried material, either purchased or your own stored herbs, crumble them between your hands. Use a mortar and pestle to bruise seeds and crush roots. If you buy herbs for this purpose, buy them in a cut and sifted form whenever possible, rather than whole or powdered.

Fill jars at least three-quarters full if herbs are fresh, leaving at least an inch clearance at the top. The finer you chop the herbs, the lower their level should be in the jar. If you're using dried herbs, fill the jar only halfway. Add the liquid as described on the following pages.

Fill jar ¾ full with fresh herbs for an extraction.

Storing. Herbal solutions made with water are intended for immediate use. Keep solutions made with other solvents in a cool dark place, shake or stir them daily, and allow them to steep for about 10 days, until the liquid extracts the virtues of the herbs — that is, the chemicals soluble in that particular liquid. You can use the extracted herbal solution either directly or blended first with other ingredients, like soap.

The basic recipes that follow describe the various ways to make herbal extractions, such as solar infusions and decoctions. When you follow one of the specific cleaning formula recipes in Chapter 5, it will specify what type of extraction you need to start with.

A Jar of Herbs

For all extractions, use a wide-mouthed glass jar with a lid that seals tightly. Don't use a two-piece lid, because it will leak as you shake the jar. Solutions containing vinegar should be sealed with plastic rather than metal lids, as the vinegar reacts with metal.

Beginner's Guide to Herbal Housekeeping

Infusions

An infusion is created by steeping herbs in water to release the herbs' water-soluble components. Because herbal solutions for cleaning should be strong, you'll need much larger quantities for a cleaning infusion than you would to make a tea for drinking. The amounts given below assume that you'll be using a quart jar to make your infusion. Adjust all amounts if you use a different-sized container. Be sure the container you use is heat-proof. My favorite piece of equipment for making infusions and decoctions is an old Pyrex coffeepot with a lid. The spout makes it easy to pour the liquid through a strainer.

Cold infusions are not recommended for housework, as they allow for continued breeding of any bacteria or other microscopic life forms on the herbs.

BASIC METHOD FOR MAKING AN INFUSION

1. Place herbs in a container.
2. Boil water, and pour it over the herbs, filling the container to within an inch or two of the top. Stir rapidly with a stainless-steel spoon or fork, just to be sure the herbs are fully saturated. Put on the lid and allow to steep for at least 15 minutes.
3. Strain and use immediately while the infusion is still hot, especially if you're planning to add soap. Otherwise, refrigerate it for use within a few days. To use later, heat it up on the stove or in the microwave oven, but do not bring to a boil.

What You Need

2 cups dried herb flowers and/or leaves, crumbled (3 cups fresh, chopped)

3–3½ cups water

Pour boiling water over fresh herbs.

Decoctions

A decoction is created by simmering tougher plant materials, such as roots, barks, seeds, peels, and fruits, to release the chemicals from the plants.

BASIC METHOD FOR MAKING A DECOCTION

1. Place fresh plant material and 3 cups of water in a heat-proof container, and bring to a simmer. (With dried material, use 5 cups of water. You can double or triple these amounts, proportionally, if desired.)
2. Simmer until the water is reduced by half. Keep an eye on the pot, and do not allow the water to evaporate too much. Scorched herbs smell awful!
3. Strain and use the decoction immediately while it's still hot, especially if you're planning to add soap. Otherwise, refrigerate it and use it within a few days. To use later, reheat it on the stove or in the microwave.

What You Need

1 cup roots, barks, seeds, peels, or fruits

3–5 cups water

Add herbs and simmer until water reduces by half.

Decoction-Infusion Combination

This method works well when you want to combine delicate materials like mint, which cannot tolerate boiling, with something tougher, like pine bark, that requires boiling.

BASIC METHOD FOR MAKING A DECOCTION-INFUSION COMBINATION

1. Place roots, barks, seeds, peels, or fruits and 3 cups of water in a heat-proof container, and bring the mixture to a simmer. (With dried plant material, use 5 cups of water.)

2. Simmer until the water is reduced by half. Watch carefully and do not allow water to evaporate too much.
3. Remove from heat. Add delicate leaves and flowers. Stir well. Add additional hot water, if necessary.
4. Cover and allow to steep for at least 15 minutes.
5. Strain and use immediately while the mixture is still hot, especially if you're planning to add soap. Otherwise, refrigerate it for use within a few days. To use later, reheat it on the stove or in the microwave oven, but do not boil.

> **What You Need**
>
> 1 cup roots, barks, seeds, peels, or fruits
> 1 cup flowers and/or leaves
> 3–5 cups water

Vinegar Extraction

I make more herbal cleaning solutions with vinegar than with any other solvent. Be sure each jar has a tightly sealed, nonmetal lid that won't react with the vinegar. You can purchase inexpensive plastic lids that fit standard-sized canning jars. The amounts given here assume that you'll be using a quart jar to make your extraction.

If you're in a hurry, you can speed the process by heating the vinegar and pouring the hot vinegar onto the herbs. You can simply steep for at least 15 minutes, then strain and use, but it is better to allow the herbs to steep in the vinegar for at least a few days.

BASIC METHOD FOR MAKING A VINEGAR EXTRACTION

1. Place herbs in jar.
2. Fill the jar with vinegar. Be sure all herbs are covered completely. Use a stainless-steel fork or spoon to press down the herbs into the liquid if necessary. Tighten the lid and shake the jar.
3. Put the jar in a cool, dark place for about 10 days. Check it within

> **What You Need**
>
> 2 cups dried herb flowers and/or leaves, crumbled (3 cups fresh, chopped)
> 3–3½ cups vinegar

Household Herbs

the first 24 hours and add more vinegar if herbs have swelled above the level of the liquid. Shake occasionally.
4. After 10 days, strain into a narrow-mouthed bottle. Label, and use as needed.

Alcohol Extraction

Because you are using potable grain alcohol, isopropyl alcohol, or denatured grain alcohol, never heat this mixture, as it can spontaneously combust or explode. (See page 71 for information about alcohol types and their uses.) The amounts given on the following page assume that you will be using a quart jar to make your extraction. If your container is a different size, adjust the recipe proportionally.

BASIC METHOD FOR MAKING AN ALCOHOL EXTRACTION

1. Place herbs in jar.
2. Fill the jar with alcohol. Be sure all herbs are covered completely. Use a stainless-steel fork or spoon to press down the herbs into the liquid if necessary. Tighten the lid and shake the jar.
3. Put the jar in a cool, dark place for about 10 days. Check it within 24 hours and add more alcohol if herbs have swelled above the level of the liquid. Shake occasionally.
4. After 10 days, strain into a narrow-mouthed bottle. Label, and use as needed.

What You Need

2 cups dried herb flowers and/or leaves (3 cups fresh)

3–3½ cups alcohol

Cover herbs with alcohol.

Ammonia Extraction

Do not heat ammonia on the stove; its fumes are too intense. The amounts given here assume that you're using a quart jar for your extraction; adjust them proportionally if you use a different-sized container.

Beginner's Guide to Herbal Housekeeping

BASIC METHOD FOR MAKING AN AMMONIA EXTRACTION

What You Need

2 cups dried herb flowers and/or leaves (3 cups fresh)

3–3½ cups ammonia

1. Place herbs in jar.
2. Fill the jar with ammonia. Be sure all herbs are covered completely. Use a stainless-steel fork or spoon to press down the herbs into the liquid if necessary. Tighten the lid and shake the jar.
3. Put the jar in a cool, dark place for about 10 days. Check it within 24 hours and add more ammonia if herbs have swelled above the level of the liquid. Shake occasionally.
4. Strain into a narrow-mouthed bottle. Label, and use as needed.

Glycerin Extraction (Glycerates)

Glycerin will extract more herbal components if you dilute it with 190-proof alcohol, at a rate of 1 part alcohol to 10 parts glycerin (1 tablespoon plus 2 teaspoons of alcohol per cup of glycerin). If you plan to use this solution as a soak to restore flexibility to brittle plastic containers or vinyl shower curtains, however, don't dilute the glycerin with alcohol. The amounts given here assume that you're using a quart jar for the extraction.

BASIC METHOD FOR MAKING A GLYCERIN EXTRACTION

What You Need

1 cup dried herb flowers and/or leaves (3 cups fresh)

3–3½ cups glycerin

1. Place herbs in jar.
2. Fill the jar with glycerin. Be sure all herbs are covered completely. Use a stainless-steel fork or spoon to press down the herbs into the liquid if necessary. Tighten the lid and shake the jar.
3. Put the jar in a cool, dark place for about 10 days. Check it within the first 24 hours and add more glycerin if herbs have swelled above the level of the liquid. Shake occasionally.
4. After 10 days, strain the mixture into a narrow-mouthed bottle. Label, and use as needed.

Quality Control

How can you judge the quality of an herbal extract? As much as possible, it should smell recognizably of the fresh or dried herbs in it, combined with the scent of the extract agent, when vinegar, ethyl alcohol, glycerin, or oil is used. You shouldn't detect off odors, rankness, rot, or rancidity. (The exceptions are herbs extracted in ammonia or isopropyl alcohol; both have such a pungent scent that it's very difficult to smell the herbs in them.)

Oil Extraction (Infused Oil)

Homemade infused oils are extractions created by saturating plant material in a nonvolatile oil in order to withdraw all the oil-soluble components. They are very different from essential oils, which are concentrated compounds produced under lab conditions (see page 72). To make infused oils, use powdered or pulverized dried herbs. Because fresh herbs contain water, they tend to turn the herbal oil rancid.

Infused oils probably require the most work of any herbal extraction method. Straining is a particular challenge. The particles must be removed completely to avoid bacterial contamination. You can let the herbal residue ("marc") settle and then siphon off the oil using tubing, or you can strain the solution. The more traditional method below is followed by a shortcut process on page 84.

BASIC METHOD FOR MAKING INFUSED OIL

1. Put the herbs in a wide-mouthed jar.
2. Add the oils, stirring carefully. Add enough oil so that the herbs are completely covered and there is ½ inch of oil above the top of the herbs.
3. Tighten the lid, and place the jar in a dark, warm place for 10 days, checking

What You Need

2 cups dried herb flowers and/or leaves

About 3 cups oil (mineral, olive, or jojoba)

¾ teaspoon vitamin E oil (to prevent rancidity)

after the first 24 hours and adding more oil if necessary. Shake or stir daily.

4. To siphon off the oil, use clean, clear, ¼-inch plastic tubing (available at home centers). Put one end of the tubing in the jar of infused oil with the herbs. Suck gently on the end of the tube until the oil starts flowing, then thrust the end into a cup placed below the level of the jar.
5. Strain the oil through a fine-mesh tea strainer.

Siphon off the infused oil into a vessel placed at a lower level.

SHORTCUT METHOD FOR MAKING INFUSED OIL

1. Combine the herbs and oil in the top of a double boiler.
2. Heat to 100°F, and maintain this temperature for 6 hours. Allow to cool.
3. Strain into a glass jar. Add the vitamin E oil. Use immediately.

What You Need

1 cup powdered dried herbs
1 cup oil (mineral, olive, or jojoba)
¼ teaspoon vitamin E oil

Dark, Warm Storage Areas

Herbalists sometimes have to be creative to find warm spots in which to make their infused oils. Some place the jars in brown paper bags and leave them in the sun for 10 days; others I know bury their jars in a sandbox. Some put them on top of their refrigerator, while others use a heating pad or an electric yogurt maker to create a consistently warm environment.

Household Herbs

CHAPTER 4

HERBAL
Housekeeping
Recipes

aking your own housekeeping solutions is simple, easy, and rewarding. When you use the scents of your favorite herbs and essential oils, you'll find that your most tedious chores are almost sublime — or at least, they're more enjoyable than working with chemically scented products. The herbs and essential oils add much more than fragrance, too. They actually cut greases, attract dust, fight bacteria, and stimulate the immune system, naturally, while lifting your spirits as you work. I recommend my favorite herbs and essential oils for making these products, but you may find others that work equally well. As you become more experienced, you'll find it's easy to substitute your own favorites for those used here.

In this chapter you'll find recipes for all of your household cleaning needs, from laundry soaps to kitchen and bathroom cleaners to safe and gentle products for the nursery. You'll want to refer to Chapter 3 for complete directions on how to prepare infusions, extractions, and other basic techniques that are part of these recipes. And examine the charts on herbal housekeeping ingredients, essential oils, and fixatives, beginning on page 120, for information about any unfamiliar ingredients in these recipes.

SCOURING POWDERS

Use scouring powders, along with a helping of elbow grease, to remove tough grime on hard surfaces like counter tops, porcelain fixtures, and wall tile. The essential oils speed things up by dissolving greasy dirt and disinfecting surfaces. Scouring powders vary in abrasiveness depending on which minerals (such as chalk, baking soda, borax, salt, or washing soda) you use. If you prefer soft scrubbers, each recipe explains how to make a paste variation.

Storage. Store the powders in a metal or glass shaker, sealing holes with aluminum foil to prevent the oils from evaporating between uses. (See Super Shakers below for storage ideas.)

Super Shakers

A #2 glass honey jar makes an ideal shaker for homemade scouring powders. Its striated sides make it easy to grip and its wide mouth makes filling it a breeze. To safely make a few holes in the plastic lid, lay the lid top-side-down on a piece of scrap wood. Then use a drill with a ⅛- or 3/16-inch drill bit to make a few holes in it. Drill metal lids the same way, or pierce them using a hammer and nail.

Low-Abrasion Scouring Powder

Low-abrasion formulas are safe for fiberglass and the plastics used in appliances. This recipe and those that follow can be modified to make an easy-to-use paste by adding liquid soap to the powder.

> 1½ cups chalk
> 4–4½ teaspoons essential oils (see below for suggestions)

1. Wearing a dust mask, place the chalk in a bowl. Add the essential oils. Using a wire whisk, thoroughly blend the oils into the powder.
2. Apply with a dampened sponge, or for more abrasive power, use a loofah, ayate cloth (a coarse natural-fiber scrubber), or Teflon scrubber pad.

PERSONAL FAVORITES

Bracing Fresh Scent: 2 teaspoons lavender oil, 1½ teaspoons spruce or fir oil, and ½ teaspoon eucalyptus oil

Citrus Scrubber: 1½ teaspoons each grapefruit, lemon, and orange oils. If you prefer, use tangerine oil in place of any or all of these citrus oils.

Low-Abrasion Soft Scrubber Paste

To make a soft scrubber paste, add ¾ cup liquid soap (such as Dr. Bronner's Liquid Lavender Castile Soap) to the Low-Abrasion Scouring Powder.

Gentle Scouring Powder

Use this scouring powder to remove greasy dirt from appliances, porcelain fixtures, tile floors, and stainless-steel sinks. The baking soda, while gentle, is a bit more abrasive than the low-abrasion chalk formula above.

> 1½ cups baking soda
> 4½ teaspoons essential oils (see below for suggestions)

Herbal Housekeeping Recipes

1. Wearing a dust mask, place the baking soda in a bowl. Add the essential oils, and use a wire whisk to blend them thoroughly into the powder.
2. Apply with a dampened sponge, or for more abrasive power, use a loofah, ayate cloth, or Teflon scrubber pad.

PERSONAL FAVORITES

Citrus and Mint: 1 tablespoon tangerine essential oil and 1 teaspoon spearmint essential oil

Lavender and Rosemary: 1 tablespoon lavender essential oil and 1 teaspoon rosemary essential oil

> **Gentle Soft Scrubber**
>
> For a light- to medium-duty soft scrubber, add ¾ cup liquid soap (such as Dr. Bronner's Liquid Lavender Castile Soap) to the basic powder. Use a funnel to get the mixture into a plastic squeeze bottle. Be sure to label clearly, as it looks a bit like cake frosting.

Heavy-Duty Scouring Powder

Use this heavy-duty scouring powder on dirty or stained toilets, tubs, ovens, and nonaluminum pots and pans. Avoid getting this powder on grout, however, as the washing soda may react with the grout and weaken it.

½ cup baking soda
½ cup borax
½ cup washing soda
4½ teaspoons essential oils (see page 93 for suggestions)

1. Wearing a dust mask, combine baking soda, borax, and washing soda in bowl. Add the essential oils, and using a whisk, blend the oils thoroughly into the powder.
2. Apply with a sponge; for more abrasive power, use a loofah, ayate cloth, or Teflon scrubber pad.

> **Heavy-Duty Scrubber Paste**
>
> For a heavy-duty scrubber paste, add ¾ to 1 cup liquid soap (such as Dr. Bronner's Liquid Peppermint Castile Soap). Be sure to label the container; this mixture looks just like grated Parmesan cheese!

PERSONAL FAVORITE

Minty-Fresh Blend: 1 tablespoon peppermint oil, 1 teaspoon anise oil, and ½ teaspoon clove oil

Toilet Bowl Cleaner

To make a toilet bowl cleaner out of the Gentle Scouring Powder (page 87), sprinkle about ½ cup of the scouring powder into the toilet, spray with any herbal vinegar to create a bubbling paste, and use a brush to scour. Or, sprinkle Heavy-Duty Scouring Powder (page 88) in the toilet and leave overnight. In the morning, spray with an herbal vinegar and scrub.

SURFACE CLEANERS

Use the scouring powders and soft scrubbers on pages 87–88 for kitchen counter tops, appliances, painted walls, vinyl or ceramic tile, and other hard, impermeable surfaces. To clean light soil on walls, cabinets, counter tops, and floors, add 2 tablespoons of borax or 1 to 2 tablespoons of castile soap to 1 gallon of hot water or hot herb infusion.

Heavy-Duty Cleaner

When your cleaning tasks need a bit more power, mix up this formula. You can also use a combination of washing soda and borax, in equal amounts.

> 1–2 tablespoons essential oil (see below for suggestions)
> ½–1 cup herb-infused ammonia or
> ¼–½ cup washing soda or borax
> 1 gallon (or more) herb-infused or plain hot water

1. Combine essential oil with ammonia, washing soda, or borax in a bucket.
2. Add hot water.

Storage. Use mixture immediately.

Herbal Vinegar to the Rescue

To disinfect, spray herbal vinegar or alcohol extractions directly on surfaces, leave on for at least 10 minutes, then wipe off. Or, use ¼ cup vinegar or alcohol in 1 gallon of rinse water.

PERSONAL FAVORITES

General: Lavender essential oil
Flea control: Orange essential oil
Disinfecting and energizing: Peppermint essential oil

Essential Oil–Enhanced Liquid Castile Soap

The glycerin in this formula acts as a solvent for the essential oil; it is also an emulsifier, blending the essential oil and the soap. Dilute this product to clean fine hand-washables, counter tops, lightly soiled walls, floors, and fixtures. It's very safe and nontoxic.

> 1 tablespoon essential oil (see page 91 for suggestions)
> 1 tablespoon glycerin
> 1 cup scented or unscented Dr. Bronner's Liquid Castile Soap

1. Combine the essential oil with the glycerin in a small bowl. Blend them thoroughly before adding the mixture to the soap. Adding essential oil to liquid soap without glycerin causes curdling.
2. Add the essential oil and glycerin mixture to the soap. Stir well to blend. Pour into a labeled glass or plastic bottle.

Use. Add 1 tablespoon to a basin of warm water for fine hand-washables, or ¼ cup or more to machine wash. Use ¼ to 1 cup of herbal vinegar in the rinse water to remove soap residue.

Storage. Store in a glass jar for a year or more, or in plastic for 6 months to 1 year.

Cleaning Marble

Use mildly alkaline soaps to wash marble, such as Essential Oil–Enhanced Liquid Castile Soap (above) and Essential Oil–Enhanced Murphy's Soap (page 91). Avoid vinegar solutions, because the acid can damage the surface.

PERSONAL FAVORITES

Orange, tangerine, lemon, grapefruit, fir, spruce, and lavender are all good choices and relatively inexpensive essential oils, although you can try more expensive ones, as well.

Essential Oil-Enhanced Murphy's Soap

This is my favorite soap for cleaning semipermeable surfaces like wood floors, painted walls, shellacked woodwork, and varnished furniture. Its ability to clean and disinfect is enhanced when essential oils are added. For woodwork and furniture, I like to complete the job with Duster's Delight (page 98).

> 4 cups Murphy's Oil Soap Concentrate (available at paint stores)
> 8 tablespoons essential oil (see below for suggestions)

1. Measure the soap concentrate into a glass jar.
2. Add essential oils and beat thoroughly with a paddle or flat spoon to disperse them completely.

Use. Add about 1 tablespoon of the mixture to a quart of hot, strained herb infusion. Whisk to a froth. Apply with a sponge or soft cloth. Rinse with ½ cup herbal vinegar in 1 gallon water (for woodwork, I like citrus peel vinegar). Wipe dry if you follow this treatment with Duster's Delight.

Storage. Store concentrate in a glass jar for a year or more.

PERSONAL FAVORITE

5 tablespoons lavender essential oil, 2 tablespoons orange essential oil, and 1 tablespoon rosemary essential oil

GLASS CLEANERS

Window-washing equipment is standard fare: a spray bottle for the solution, lots of huck toweling or other lint-free cotton or linen rags (like old dish towels or cotton-knit T-shirts) to clean with, and a chamois or clean, dry cloths for the final polish.

Herbal Housekeeping Recipes

Herbal Vinegar Window and Mirror Wash

For sparkling clean windows, vinegar solutions have no equal. If you use herb infusions with insect-repellent qualities, you'll discourage flies and mosquitoes from clustering at your windows.

>   3 cups water
>   ¼ cup, plus 2 tablespoons herbal vinegar, strained
>   (see below for suggestions)

1. Pour the water into a spray bottle.
2. Add herbal vinegar. Shake well. Label.
Use. Spray on windows, then polish with a clean, dry cloth.
Storage. Store in a spray bottle. Keeps for about 6 months.

PERSONAL FAVORITES
Fragrant herbs: Anise hyssop, basil, bay, eucalyptus, hyssop, lavender, marjoram, oregano, rosemary, roses, sage, sweet Annie, sweet grass, winter savory
Bug-repellent herbs: Epazoté, southernwood, sweet Annie, tansy, wormwood, yarrow

Glass Scratch Remover

Try this scratch remover for fine scratches. If you have a deep scratch, try Cerium Oxide Polishing Powder (for suppliers, see "Glaziers," in your Yellow Pages).

>   1 tablespoon herb infusion
>   1 tablespoon plain glycerin or herbal glycerate
>   1–2 tablespoons powdered chalk

1. Combine the herb infusion with the glycerin in a small bowl.
2. Add drops of the liquid to the powdered chalk, stirring until a thick paste forms. (You may not need all the liquid.)
Use. Apply with a soft cloth, burnishing at right angles to scratch. Rinse. Repeat if needed. This formula is intended for immediate use.

Window Screens

Wash screens with an herbal castile soap or Essential Oil–Enhanced Murphy's Soap (see page 91), and allow to dry. Spray with a bug-repellent herb infusion made with any of the following herbs: bay, bee balm, calamus, epazoté, ginkgo, hyssop, mugwort, sage, southernwood, sweet Annie, sweet grass, tansy, wormwood, or yarrow.

You can also use a diluted herbal isopropyl alcohol for this, but try a test area before spraying the entire screen, to make sure it doesn't damage the screening material.

METAL POLISHES

Lustrous, glowing metals are attractive, welcoming elements of every gracious home. The nontoxic polishes in this section will have you smiling happily while you bring a bright glowing sheen to brass, silver, and other household metals.

Aluminum Polish

To clean the inside of an aluminum pan, pour any undiluted herb vinegar into it, and simmer over low heat for 10–60 minutes, until all discoloration disappears. Discard the vinegar afterward. To clean small aluminum items, put them in a saucepan, cover them with herb vinegar, and simmer over low heat until they are clean. (Use aluminum, enameled steel, enameled cast-iron, or stainless-steel pans for this purpose. Do not use cast iron, which reacts with the vinegar, not only interfering with the cleaning process, but affecting the seasoning of the pan, as well.)

Paste-style aluminum polish. For non-submersible items or for extra power, mix about ¼ cup citric acid with enough herbal vinegar to create a sticky paste, and rub on. (Don't use baking soda or washing soda solutions to clean aluminum as they will dull it.)

Herbal Housekeeping Recipes

Brass Polish

Clean lacquered brass with mild soap and water. For unlacquered brass, dampen the object with vinegar (or equal parts of vinegar and isopropyl alcohol), sprinkle with salt, and scour with a Teflon-safe abrasive pad moistened with vinegar. Add more salt, if needed.

Paste-style brass polish. Combine ¼ cup chalk with enough herbal vinegar to make a paste. For more acidity, blend 1–2 tablespoons citric acid with the chalk, or combine Gentle Soft Scrubber (page 88) with herb-infused isopropyl alcohol.

Chrome and Stainless-Steel Polish

Use herb vinegar or herb-infused isopropyl alcohol to clean all chrome and stainless steel. This is especially good for cleaning car chrome in the winter, as it doesn't freeze.

Paste-style chrome and stainless-steel polish. For mild abrasion, mix ¼ cup chalk with enough alcohol to create a sticky paste. (As alcohol prevents water spotting, it's better than vinegar for use on chrome. To get rid of soap scum, however, combine chalk with vinegar, or use vinegar alone.) Or, use Low-Abrasion Soft Scrubber Paste (page 87).

Copper Polish

Dampen the copper item, sprinkle it with salt, and then spray with any herbal vinegar, especially citrus peel vinegar. Rub with an abrasive pad or the cut surface of half a lemon or lime. (Lime is more acidic than lemon, so it works faster). Rinse well and dry.

Silver Polish

Low-Abrasion Soft Scrubber Paste (page 87) made with Bracing Fresh Air essential oils makes a wonderful silver polish. Apply with a soft cloth or chamois. Rinse well and dry immediately. Gentle Soft Scrubber (page 88) works almost as well.

CARPET AND RUG CLEANERS

Carpets and rugs are soft underfoot and muffle sounds, making our homes quiet refuges from the outer world. Unfortunately, they also attract and hold dust, dirt, odors, and microorganisms, all of which exacerbate allergies. The recipes in this section are designed to deodorize carpeting, remove stains, and discourage fleas and other insects.

Herb-and-Baking Soda Refresher

This herbal powder whisks away odors from carpets. Purchase powdered herbs, or pulverize herbs in a coffee grinder or spice mill. (Clean the coffee mill first by whirling dry bread crumbs in it, and discard the first batch of herbs if they smell of coffee.) For light-colored carpets, use ½ tablespoon of essential oil per 1 cup of baking soda instead of herbs, or use crumbled rather than powdered herbs. If the carpeting smells very bad, pretreat before using this refresher. First, remove any stains (see Essential–Oil Ammonia Treatment for Carpets below, and Rosemary and Fuller's Earth Grease Remover on page 107), then use powdered zeolite according to the package directions.

> 2½ cups each powdered roses, powdered lavender, powdered rosemary, and powdered sandalwood
> 10 cups baking soda

1. Blend all the ingredients together thoroughly.
2. Vacuum the rug, then sprinkle refresher onto the carpet and spread it with a natural bristle brush. Leave it overnight or for several days, then vacuum. Avoid walking on the carpet during treatment.

Essential Oil–Ammonia Treatment for Carpets

Full-strength orange or rosemary essential oils remove grease from wool carpeting. For other stains, make this ammonia–essential oil formula. Although the solution, as well as undiluted essential oils, is safe for wool carpets, it may damage the carpet padding, so place an absorbent pad between the carpet and foam pad before treating, if

Herbal Housekeeping Recipes

possible. If the carpet is made from synthetic fibers, check with the manufacturer or test an unobtrusive area before treating. For stain removal, use regular ammonia rather than herb-infused ammonia, which may discolor the carpet.

Safety first. *Open a window for ventilation during this treatment.*

> ½–4 tablespoons orange or rosemary essential oil
> 1 cup ammonia
> 1 cup cool water

1. Combine the essential oil, ammonia, and water in a glass spray bottle. Shake well.
2. Place an absorbent cloth between the carpet and carpet pad, directly under the stain.
3. Spray the stain heavily, then dab with another absorbent cloth to pick up the stain residue. Continue spraying and dabbing until the stain is gone. (Shake the solution vigorously before each application.)
4. Remove the absorbent cloth from between the carpet and carpet pad, and replace it with a clean dry cloth.
5. Sprinkle bentonite (see page 120), borax, or baking soda on the spot to absorb any remaining liquid. Allow the powder to sit on the carpet until it is completely dry, then vacuum the residue. Avoid walking on the treated area until it has been vacuumed. Remove the cloth from under the treated area.

Orange Peel and Boric Acid Treatment for Fleas

To make this flea treatment even more effective, add ¼–1 pound of diatomaceous earth to the powder. This powder is intended to be left in place, except on carpets (both boric acid and diatomaceous earth can damage fibers) and in high traffic areas.

> 1 pound granulated orange peel
> 1 pound boric acid
> ¼ pound powdered calamus root
> ¼ pound powdered painted daisy (pyrethrum daisy) flower buds
> 1 ounce orange essential oil (optional)

1. Vacuum the area to be treated.
2. Combine the orange peel, boric acid, calamus root, and flower buds. Stir in the orange essential oil, if desired.
3. *For flea control,* sprinkle under couch cushions, on carpeting under furniture, along baseboards, under beds, between mattresses and box springs, and anywhere fleas may be hiding. *For roach control,* put some under the kitchen sink, inside cabinets, and on pantry shelves. Leave overnight, then vacuum traffic areas.

Storage. Store in a carefully labelled glass jar or metal container for up to 6 months.

Safety first. *Wear a dust mask while blending and applying powders containing boric acid or diatomaceous earth. Pregnant women should not use essential oil of pennyroyal. Some people develop a rash from pyrethrum flowers, so wear gloves when you work with this powder. Keep this powder away from small children.*

FURNITURE AND WOODWORK CLEANERS AND POLISHES

I love the warmth and beauty of wood cabinets, moldings, and furniture, which add so much to the ambiance of a gracious, welcoming home. These cleaning formulas enhance wood's natural beauty.

Wood-Washing Formula

Use this formula to wash wood surfaces, including floors, cabinets, and woodwork, whenever they need it. The ingredients are safe enough to use weekly.

½ cup dried herbs, such as lemon balm, lemon thyme, sweet cicely, costmary, and/or lavender
1 cup water
½ cup Essential Oil–Enhanced Murphy's Soap (page 91)
1 gallon water
½ cup citrus peel vinegar

Herbal Housekeeping Recipes 97

1. Make an infusion with the herbs, and steep for 15 minutes. Strain.
2. Add Essential Oil–Enhanced Murphy's Soap to the hot infusion, and whisk to dissolve. If the solution has cooled too much to dissolve the soap, heat the mixture in a microwave oven or double boiler. Apply the soap solution with a sponge or soft cloth.
3. In a bucket, combine 1 gallon of water with the citrus peel vinegar. Use the solution as a rinse, then wipe dry.

Using Essential Oils on Wood

Essential oils add fragrance, luster, and bacteria-bashing qualities to each of the following formulas.

Dusting Polish. Open windows wide. With a spray bottle, apply lemon, rosemary, lavender, or other essential oil to a lamb's-wool duster, and use on shellacked or varnished woodwork and furniture. Do only one room or object per day, as the fragrance is quite intense. Test before using any undiluted essential oil on painted woodwork. You can dilute by using 1¼ cups of mineral or jojoba oil to 1 tablespoon of essential oil.

Duster's Delight. Mix up to 1 tablespoon of lemon or other essential oil into ¼ cup of mineral oil, then combine with 1 cup Citra-Solv in a spray bottle. Before applying, damp-mop the surface with water and a splash of herbal vinegar. Spray a clean dust mop with Duster's Delight, and dust the surface. Lamb's-wool dusters or light-colored, recycled wool sweaters make the best mops, as they attract dust effectively.

Fragrant Oil Finish. Mix together 1½ teaspoons of balsam of Peru essential oil and 1½ teaspoons of other essential oils (such as citrus, evergreen, and lavender), then combine with 1 cup of mineral or jojoba oil. Apply to unfinished (or unvarnished, but oiled) wood furniture with soft, lint-free rags. Allow to soak in. Wipe off excess, if required. Reapply if necessary, especially to the end grain of the wood. For a more resistant finish, follow with Fragrant Wood Furniture Polish (page 99) or Fragrant Furniture and Floor Wax (page 99).

Fragrant Wood Furniture Polish

This wax with the pleasant vanilla fragrance of balsam of Peru not only protects wood surfaces, especially unfinished wood, but it's also a pleasure to use. For a stiffer wax, increase the amount of beeswax to 2 ounces. For a harder wax that can be buffed, use 1–1½ ounces paraffin or carnauba wax (see page 120) instead of the beeswax.

>   1 ounce beeswax
>   1 cup mineral or jojoba oil
>   1½ teaspoons balsam of Peru essential oil
>   1½ teaspoons other essential oils (see below for suggestions)

1. Melt the beeswax in the oil in the top of a double boiler. Remove from heat and allow to cool just until a crescent of wax forms at the edge of the pan.

2. Add balsam of Peru and other essential oils. Stir well.

Use. *For unfinished or oil-finished wood,* use this solution while it is still liquid, as this gives the best penetration. Use a paintbrush or lamb's-wool pad to apply. Rub in well and allow to cool.

For varnished or shellacked wood, apply the cooled solution with a soft, lint-free rag, then buff well.

Storage. Store excess furniture polish in a labelled glass jar indefinitely.

🌿 PERSONAL FAVORITES
Sandalwood, rosewood, balsam of tolu, tangerine, grapefruit, and lemon

Fragrant Furniture and Floor Wax

Floor wax is usually made with a solvent like mineral spirits. Once applied to the wood, the solvent evaporates, leaving behind the hard wax to protect the floor or furniture. Because mineral spirits, a petroleum derivative, may cause health problems, the following recipes substitute an ingredient for the mineral spirits: Citra-Solv (a commercial product made from essential oil components) and turpentine (a volatile essential oil distilled from resin taken from coniferous trees, especially longleaf pines). If you'd like to make a harder mixture that you can buff, substitute paraffin or carnauba for the beeswax, and use 4 ounces of beeswax to 1 cup of Citra-Solv.

> 5 ounces beeswax
> 1 cup Citra-Solv
> 1 tablespoon lemon or tangerine essential oil

1. Melt the wax in a double boiler on low heat. When it has completely melted, remove from heat.
2. Add the Citra-Solv. Stir well. Allow to cool slightly.
3. Add the essential oil.
4. Carefully pour the wax into a jar. Label and allow it to cool before using. It will set up to a very soft paste.

Use. Apply with a soft cloth or lamb's-wool pad; buff. Waxing should be done only once a year. In between waxings, wash and dry-mop wood floors with Duster's Delight (page 98).

Storage. Store in a glass jar in a cool, dark place; it keeps for years.

Safe Use of Solvents

Solvents are combustible, so take these precautions with them:
- Most important, melt the wax first, remove it from the heat, and then pour in the solvent. *Never* heat the solvent. The fumes are very strong and the potential for a fire is great.
- When heating the wax, use a double boiler over a low flame.
- Keep the vent hood of your stove top running.
- Have a fire extinguisher nearby.
- Don't leave the room during the process.
- Waxy rags can spontaneously combust, so dispose of them properly. If in doubt, check with your local fire department.
- Don't machine-wash rags coated with waxes or solvents, as there's a chance that a spark from the electrical system could ignite the fumes from the solvents.

Laundry Aids

Laundry has a lot in common with death and taxes. They all seem to be inevitable. Here are my solutions for the ever-present laundry pile. I'm sorry I can't do anything about the other two.

Delicate Fabric Froth

Yucca or soapwort roots clean fine fabrics, antique baskets, tapestries, hats, and other textiles that should not be immersed in water, as well as lightly soiled natural-fiber upholstery fabrics and Oriental rugs.

¼ cup powdered dry yucca root or soapwort root
3 cups water

1. Put yucca or soapwort roots in the bottom of a blender. Boil water, then pour it over the powdered roots. With the lid on the blender, run on high for 2 or 3 minutes, or until froth no longer increases. Allow mixture to settle before removing the lid. To avoid gritty roots permeating the suds, don't pour the liquid out of the blender.
2. Scoop out the froth with your hand or a soft brush, and gently rub it into textile. Allow suds to dry on the object, then brush or rinse off. If more froth is needed, blitz the liquid in blender again. When froth is gone, strain the liquid remaining in the blender, and use it to hand-wash silk and wool items, or even your hair.

Storage. Use immediately.

> **Dryer Scents**
>
> To scent clothes naturally, put a drop of lavender, rosemary, or any citrus essential oil on a cotton handkerchief, and toss it in the dryer near the end of the cycle.

Essential Oil-Powdered Detergent Booster

This naturally scented detergent not only smells wonderful, but the essential oil boosts your immune system as well. One detergent that works well is Arm and Hammer Perfume and Dye Free detergent.

Herbal Housekeeping Recipes

2 tablespoons orange, lavender, or rosemary essential oil
5 pounds unscented powdered laundry detergent

Combine the essential oil with the laundry detergent in a large kettle, and mix well with a heavy-duty whisk.

Use. Use the amount (or a bit less) called for on the detergent label.

Storage. Mix and store in a large kettle with a tight-fitting lid to prevent the oils from evaporating. (Although plastic containers are convenient for storage, essential oils tend to dissipate through plastic, so glass or metal is preferred.)

STAIN REMOVERS AND PRETREATMENTS

Essential oil of rosemary is my favorite stain remover, especially for grease spots. The rosemary-based formulas on the following pages are similar, but they use different liquids, depending on the stain. If it's more convenient to make a paste, combine the essential oil with the mineral first, then add enough liquid to make a paste.

Safety first. If you're pregnant, substitute lavender essential oil for rosemary. Rosemary contains some camphor, which is toxic, and therefore should be avoided during pregnancy.

Rosemary-Ammonia Stain Remover

Keep this simple solution handy for stains on any washable fabric that are caused by perspiration, urine, or vomit. Dilute the solution with an equal amount of water for silk or wool. Neutralize any acidity in fresh stains by blotting them first with baking soda.

½–4 tablespoons rosemary essential oil
1 cup ammonia

1. Combine the essential oil and ammonia in a glass spray bottle.
2. Shake well to combine. Because the oil and ammonia don't mix well, you'll need to continue shaking before and during use.

Storage. Store for a year or more in a labelled glass spray bottle.

Rosemary-Vinegar Stain Remover

This stain remover is useful for getting out many different kinds of spills, spots, and stains, including alcohol, beer, coffee, cola, fruit juice, tea, tomato juice/sauce, washable ink, and wine. Before treating any wet stains, sprinkle a heavy coating of baking soda over the spill, allow it to soak up as much liquid as possible, then apply the vinegar solution. If you're treating protein stains, such as baby formula, blood, cheese sauce, feces, milk, urine, and vomit, neutralize them by alternating this solution with ammonia. To treat ink stains, apply alcohol first, then glycerin, before using this solution.

Stain Removal Tips

- Always test formula on an inconspicuous area such as a seam or hem, especially with nonwashable fabrics.
- Blot fresh stains immediately with a clean cloth to absorb as much liquid as possible. Neutralize acid stains by sprinkling them with baking soda. Allow the baking soda to set while preparing a stain-removing solution. Vacuum or shake off baking soda before continuing the treatment.
- Start with a 3-percent solution of whatever formula you're using. If it doesn't completely remove the stain, repeat the treatment.
- If greasy dirt or stains are barely affected by the treatment, increase the amount of essential oil and/or change the carrier.
- Always use cold water when pretreating stains on fabrics. Hot water sets most stains, making them harder to remove.
- Treat acid stains, such as tomato sauce, with cold water, neutralize them with baking soda, then flush them with ammonia.
- Treat alkaline stains, such as perspiration stains, with vinegar.
- Treat greasy stains with a solvent like alcohol, glycerin, or Murphy's Oil Soap, depending on the fabric. Many stains respond to liquid detergent.
- Treat combination stains, like coffee with cream, that contain an acid, a protein, and a grease either in two steps or with a combination of two solvents.

Herbal Housekeeping Recipes

½–4 tablespoons rosemary essential oil
1 cup vinegar
1 tablespoon liquid dishwashing detergent
½ cup water

1. Combine all the ingredients in a glass spray bottle.
2. Shake to combine. Because the oil and vinegar don't mix well, you'll need to continue shaking during use. Apply to the stain, and rub gently. Allow it to set for 15 minutes, then launder.

Storage. Label and store in a glass bottle; it keeps indefinitely.

Rosemary-Alcohol Stain Remover for Grass Stains

Use this stain remover on nonwashable fabrics. It may cause dyes to run, so use a pad beneath the stain when treating. You may have to treat the entire item with the solution to maintain even color.

½–4 tablespoons rosemary essential oil
1 cup alcohol (isopropyl or ethyl)

1. Combine the ingredients in a glass spray bottle.
2. With a pad beneath the stain, spray on, then blot with a clean, dry cloth. If color runs, soak the entire item in the solution. Allow it to dry in a ventilated area before having the piece dry-cleaned.

Storage. Store for up to 1 year in a labeled glass spray bottle.

Variation for Washables

For washable fabrics, add 2 tablespoons liquid detergent to the rosemary grass stain solution. Spray on stains, and then launder.

Rosemary-Alcohol Stain Remover for Grease

Although this stain remover is designed for use on washable fabrics, it may cause dyes to run, so use a pad beneath the stain when treating. You may have to submerge the entire item in the solution in order to maintain even color.

Fuller's earth
½–4 tablespoons rosemary essential oil
1 cup alcohol (isopropyl or ethyl)

1. Cover the grease stain with fuller's earth and allow it to set while you prepare alcohol solution.
2. Combine the essential oil and alcohol in a glass spray bottle.
3. Vacuum or shake off the fuller's earth, then, with a pad beneath the stain, spray the stain with the alcohol solution. Blot with a clean, dry cloth.

Storage. Store in a labeled glass spray bottle for up to 1 year.

Rosemary-Soap Stain Remover

Hand-washables like lingerie and nylons need gentle care, but they may also have picked up stubborn stains. Mix up a batch of this formula so that it's available for everything you hand-wash.

½–4 tablespoons rosemary essential oil
½–4 tablespoons glycerin
1 cup liquid castile soap
Herbal vinegar

1. Using equal amounts of essential oil and glycerin, combine the two in a small mixing bowl.
2. Pour the oil-glycerin mix into a glass bottle, add the castile soap, and blend thoroughly.
3. Dampen the article to be cleaned, and apply the soap solution directly to the stain. Rub gently. Wash the entire article in a dilute solution of the soap. Add a splash of herbal vinegar to the rinse water to remove soap residue.

Storage. Store in a labeled glass or plastic bottle for up to 6 months.

Rosemary-Peroxide Stain Pretreatment

A pretreatment for stains on silks and wools, this formula works especially hard on perspiration stains, and lightens white and cream-colored silks and wools. (Never use chlorine bleach on silk or wool; it damages and yellows them.) For perspiration stains on cotton, lay the garment in the sun all day, spraying it several times to keep it damp.

> ½ tablespoon rosemary essential oil
> 1 cup hydrogen peroxide

1. Combine the essential oil and peroxide in a glass spray bottle.
2. Shake well before and during use. Spray on stain until quite wet, and allow it to sit for ½ hour. After treatment, launder, adding herbal vinegar to the final rinse.

Storage. Hydrogen peroxide loses its potency within a month of being opened, so make only what you can use within that time.

Rosemary-Murphy's Stain Pretreatment

A good pretreatment for greasy stains on washable fabrics, this combination is also an excellent soap for washing goose-down pillows and comforters.

> ½–4 tablespoons rosemary essential oil
> 1 cup Murphy's Oil Soap

1. Combine the essential oil with Murphy's Oil Soap in a glass jar.
2. Apply to grease stains or combination stains on washable fabrics.

Rosemary-Glycerin Variations

For coffee, tea, and other tannin stains on nonwashable fabrics, combine this solution with an equal amount of isopropyl alcohol. Before treating, test for color fastness on a seam. Place an absorbent pad beneath the stain. Apply the solution to the stain and blot gently. Repeat if necessary. Allow to dry in an area with good air circulation, then dryclean.

For most other stains, including combinations like coffee with cream, combine 1 tablespoon of the glycerin-essential oil solution with 1 tablespoon liquid dishwashing detergent and ½ cup water. Apply directly to the stain and leave on for 15 minutes, then wash the article.

Moisten fabric first, and work the mixture into the stain. Let it set for at least 15 minutes before washing, or overnight if the stain is old.
Storage. Store for 1 year in a labeled glass bottle.

Rosemary-Lifetree Stain Pretreatment

This pretreatment works well on many types of stains on washable fabrics. Remember to use cold water when you are treating stains, as hot water sets many stains and makes them harder to remove.

> ½–4 tablespoons rosemary essential oil
> 1 cup Lifetree's Premium Dishwashing Liquid with Aloe and Calendula

1. Combine the essential oil with the dishwashing liquid in a glass spray bottle.
2. Apply to stains on dampened, washable fabrics. Scrub with a fingernail brush, if fabric is durable enough. Allow to set for 15 minutes, then launder.

Storage. Store in a labeled glass spray bottle; it keeps indefinitely.

Rosemary and Fuller's Earth Grease Remover

Use this mixture for treating grease stains on upholstery, rugs, woolen fabrics, fabrics with nap (like velvet), as well as unwashable textiles. Fuller's earth is available at hobby stores and home centers.

> ½–4 tablespoons rosemary essential oil
> 1 cup fuller's earth

1. Combine the essential oil and fuller's earth. Stir, or whirl in a blender to combine thoroughly.
2. Sprinkle the mixture onto the stain until it is fully covered. If you're cleaning a fabric with a nap, use a brush to gently work the mixture into the fibers. Allow it to set for at least 1 hour, or as long as overnight, until the grease is absorbed.
3. Vacuum, or gently dust off the mixture and discard. Repeat, if necessary.

Storage. Store in a labeled glass jar or metal container for one year.

Rosemary-Glycerin Stain Pretreatment

This is a useful pretreatment for greasy stains like butter, cooking oil, mayonnaise, or margarine on washable fabrics. See the variations below for other uses.

> ½–4 tablespoons rosemary essential oil
> 1 cup glycerin

1. Combine the essential oil and glycerin in a glass bottle.
2. Apply directly to stain and allow it to soak in. If necessary, follow the variation "for most other stains" below before laundering.

Storage. Store in a labelled glass bottle for a year or more.

LAUNDRY POWDERS AND PASTES

Essential oils add both wonderful fragrance and solvent properties to these useful laundry products. Try the powders as laundry boosters to lift dirt and grease, and mix them with water, liquid dish soap, or castile soap to make stain removal pastes for badly soiled items. Rosemary is my favorite essential oil for laundry products, but if you're pregnant, you should substitute lavender.

Rosemary and Color-Safe Bleach Presoak

Keep this formula on your laundry shelf for stains on washable colored fabrics, as well as white fabrics that you do not wish to bleach with liquid laundry bleach.

> ½–4 tablespoons rosemary essential oil
> 1 cup all-fabric bleach powder (sodium perborate)

1. Combine essential oil with bleach powder. Stir, or whirl in a blender to combine thoroughly.
2. Presoak stained fabrics in a solution containing ¼ cup of the rosemary-bleach mixture and 5 gallons of water for 1 hour. (For perspiration stains, soak overnight.) Launder, using ½–¾ cup of the rosemary-bleach mixture in the machine-wash load along with detergent.

Storage. Keeps for 6–12 months in a labeled glass jar or metal container, stored in a cool, dark place. Shake before use.

Rosemary-Baking Soda Laundry Powder

This powder goes to work to neutralize acid stains and absorb odor. If you prefer using a paste-style product (for stubborn stains or for articles that can't be laundered), add water, a few tablespoonsful at a time, to the powder mixture. Or, for an extra boost, use Lifetree's Dishwashing Liquid or another liquid detergent instead of water. Allow to dry, then remove the residue by brushing or vacuuming.

½–4 tablespoons rosemary essential oil
1 cup baking soda

1. Combine essential oil and baking soda by hand or in a blender.
2. Add ½ cup to a full washer load along with detergent.
Storage. Store in a labeled, covered glass jar or metal container; it keeps indefinitely.

Rosemary-Borax Laundry Powder

Borax works on mildew stains and neutralizes odors like urine. For difficult stains and unwashables, make a laundry paste by adding water or liquid detergent to the powder. Apply, allow to dry, then brush off the residue.

½–4 tablespoons essential oil
1 cup borax

1. Thoroughly combine essential oil and borax by hand or in a blender.
2. Add ½ cup to a full washer load along with laundry detergent.
Storage. Store in a labeled, covered glass jar or metal container; it keeps indefinitely.

Rosemary-Washing Soda Laundry Powder

This is the mixture to use for greasy dirt. If you have particularly stubborn stains or the article can't be laundered, make a laundry paste by gradually adding water or liquid detergent to the powder. Apply, allow to dry, then brush or vacuum off the residue.

> ½–4 tablespoons rosemary essential oil
> 1 cup washing soda

1. Combine essential oil and washing soda by hand or in a blender.
2. Add ½ cup to a full washer load along with detergent.
3. Add ¼ to 1 cup of herbal vinegar to the rinse water to prevent graying of whites and dulling of colors.

Storage. Store in a labeled, covered glass jar or metal container; it keeps indefinitely.

Leather Cleaners

Like all skins, leather requires frequent cleaning and moisturizing. These leather formulas can be used on the outside of suitcases, briefcases, shoes, handbags, and furniture.

Essential Oil-Enhanced Murphy's Oil Soap Concentrate for Leather

Wash leather with this solution to remove grease and grime. The stronger fragrances of roots, woods, and gums complement the scent of leather.

> 2 tablespoons of your favorite essential oil (see page 111 for suggestions)
> 1 cup Murphy's Oil Soap Concentrate (available in paint stores)
> ½ cup dried herbs (see page 111 for suggestions)
> 1½ cups water
> ¼ cup herbal vinegar
> 1 quart warm water

1. In a small bowl, stir the essential oil into the Murphy's. Beat well to disperse the oil completely.

2. Prepare an herbal infusion, using the dried herbs and 1½ cups of water. Allow to steep for 15 minutes, covered, to retain heat and fragrance. Strain into a large bowl.
3. Add 1 tablespoon of the essential oil-Murphy's mixture to the hot infusion. Whisk to a froth. Apply to leather with a sponge or soft cloth; for stiff leathers, you can use a natural bristle brush to scrub gently.
4. Rinse with a mixture of the herbal vinegar and warm water. Wipe dry with a clean cloth.

Storage. Keep the concentrated soap in a cool dark place in a labeled glass jar or metal container for up to 6 months.

PERSONAL FAVORITE

For 4 cups Murphy's Oil Soap Concentrate, use 5 tablespoons lavender essential oil, 2 tablespoons orange essential oil, and 1 tablespoon rosemary essential oil. *For the herbal infusion,* use calamus, cedarwood, rosewood, sandalwood, clary sage, patchouli, and/or lavender.

Lanolin and Murphy's Leather Treatment

Leathers need to be moisturized as well as cleaned. This formula treats dry, cracked leathers that have been badly treated, neglected, and/or improperly stored at high temperatures when wet. Lanolin is quite sticky; use the larger amount only if the leather is very dry and cracked.

> 2 tablespoons essential oil (such as lavender, orange, or rosemary)
> 1 cup Murphy's Oil Soap Concentrate
> 1–3 tablespoons lanolin

1. Combine the essential oil with the Murphy's Soap Concentrate.
2. Stir in the lanolin with a heavy spoon. The mixture will look exactly like whipped butter.
3. Rub soap mixture directly into the leather. Allow it to set for a few minutes up to an hour, while the leather softens. Work in further with your fingers or a soft brush.
4. Blend 1 tablespoon of the soap mixture with 1 quart of hot water, cool slightly, then rinse the leather.

5. If the leather is extremely dry, repeat the process, but leave the undiluted soap on the leather overnight to absorb more lanolin. Rinse with a fresh diluted soap solution, as in step 4, followed by a rinse containing ¼ cup vinegar in 1 quart of water.

Storage. Store the concentrated soap in a labeled glass jar or metal container in a cool, dark place for up to 6 months.

AIR FRESHENERS AND SWEETENERS

Nothing smells better than clean, fresh air. Here are some first-aid solutions for refreshing stale air that bring garden fragrances indoors and put them to work for you.

Vinegar Bowl

A shallow bowl containing vinegar, set out overnight in a room, is a simple, but tried-and-true method for banishing damp, musty, or smoky odors. For a fragrant herbal twist, use sweet-scented herbal vinegars, like rose, anise hyssop, sweet woodruff, or sweet grass, or raspberry vinegar and sweet grass. You can make a one-herb vinegar, called a "simple," or an herb combination. Include a fixative like sweet grass or sweet woodruff to extend the solution's life.

You can strain the solution or leave interesting fruits and flowers in the bowl. Choose a decorative, preferably flat-bottomed, shallow glass storage bowl that holds about 2 quarts of water, with a tight-fitting lid, so the solution can be used again and again.

Safety first. Don't leave the vinegar solution where small children or pets can spill it or drink from it.

- 7 cups dried herbs or 11 cups fresh herbs (see page 113 for suggestions)
- 1 gallon distilled white, cider, or other fruit-flavored vinegar
- 1 cup sweet grass or sweet woodruff, as a fixative
- 1 tablespoon allspice, cinnamon, cloves, or ginger

1. Place the herbs in a gallon jar, and pour the vinegar over them, filling the jar with liquid. Be sure all herbs are covered completely. Cover the jar. Allow to infuse for at least a week.
2. Strain, if you wish. Decant most of the vinegar into display bowl.
Use. Set the vinegar bowl on a stable surface and remove the lid. As vinegar evaporates from the bowl, add more from the storage container. Cover the bowl when its effects are not needed.
Storage. The strained vinegar lasts for several years if kept in a glass jar in a cool, dark place. If unstrained, remove any plant material that is exposed to air when the level of the liquid drops.

PERSONAL FAVORITES
Principal herb: Anise hyssop, citrus peels, costmary, eucalyptus, frankincense, fruit-scented sage, jasmine, juniper berries, lavender, lemon mint, meadowsweet, orangemint, rosemary, roses, spearmint, sweet Annie, sweet grass, sweet woodruff, or Thuja cedar leaf
Additional herbs: Chamomile, heather, lemon balm, lemon verbena, lemongrass, linden flowers, pineapple sage, or sweet Cicely

Fresh Herbal Spray

This light, refreshing spray is healthful and inexpensive to make. If you use fresh herbs, double the quantities suggested. A fixative will help the fragrance linger; try angelica or calamus root, cedarwood, oakmoss, sandalwood, sweet grass, or sweet woodruff. Avoid gummy or resinous fixatives like copal, frankincense, and myrrh, which can clog the sprayer mechanism. Calculate the amount of fixative as part of the total ½ cup of herbs. This recipe makes about ¾ cup, enough to freshen the whole house a couple of times.
Safety first. Be careful not to get spray into eyes.

> ½ cup dried herbs (see page 114 for suggestions)
> 1 cup water
> 1 or more tablespoons fixative (optional)

1. Place herbs in heat-proof container. Boil water and pour it over the herbs; stir rapidly. Cover the container and allow to steep until cool (at least ½ hour).
2. Strain. If you see bits of plant material that could clog the spray mechanism, strain again through a water-dampened paper coffee filter. Pour into a spray bottle, using a funnel if necessary.

Use. Spray into the air all around the house.

Storage. This will keep in the refrigerator for a few days.

PERSONAL FAVORITES

Lavender herb: 6 tablespoons dried lavender, 2 tablespoons dried rosemary, 10 bay leaves

Sweet rose: 6 tablespoons dried rosebuds, 2 tablespoons dried sweet woodruff

Candy-scented: 4 tablespoons dried anise hyssop, 2 tablespoons dried chamomile, 2 tablespoons dried sweet Annie, ½ teaspoon whole allspice

Light mint: 2 tablespoons dried lemon balm, 2 tablespoons dried lemon peel, 2 tablespoons dried spearmint, 2 tablespoons dried Thuja cedar leaves

Disinfectant Spray

Both the alcohol and essential oils in this herbal infusion kills microorganisms in the air and on surfaces. The more essential oil you use, the more powerful the disinfectant. I prefer to use 190-proof potable ethyl alcohol. Isopropyl alcohol is also effective, and less expensive, but its strong odor competes with the herbs. You can also use vodka, gin, or light rum.

Safety first. When made with isopropyl or denatured alcohol, this solution is toxic if ingested. Do not spray into eyes. Avoid spraying on shellacked and varnished wood surfaces, as alcohol and essential oils may mar them.

½ cup dried herbs (see page 115 for suggestions)
1 cup water

½ cup alcohol
1–2 teaspoons essential oil (see below for suggestions)

1. Make an infusion with the herbs and water, and allow to steep until cool (at least ½ hour).
2. Strain. If you see bits of plant material that could clog the spray mechanism, strain again through a water-dampened paper coffee filter. Measure out ½ cup, and set aside.
3. Place alcohol in a glass spray bottle; add the essential oils. Pour in the reserved herb infusion. Shake well.

Use. Spray into the air all around the house.
Storage. Label carefully. Keeps for 6 months — longer, if refrigerated.

PERSONAL FAVORITES

Lavender Lover: ½ cup dried lavender for the infusion; 1 to 2 teaspoons lavender essential oil

Lemon Eucalyptus: ½ cup dried eucalyptus for the infusion; 1 teaspoon lemon essential oil and 1 teaspoon lemon eucalyptus essential oil

Antiseptic Rose: ¼ cup dried roses and ¼ cup dried hyssop for the infusion; 1 teaspoon rose geranium essential oil and 1 teaspoon rosewood essential oil

Sweet Orange: 3 tablespoons each of dried anise hyssop, sweet Annie, and thyme for the infusion; 1 to 2 teaspoons orange essential oil

Moth-Away Sachets

Many herbs are moth-chasers, but unfortunately, their scents are sometimes not much more appealing to us than they are to the moths. This combination smells pretty good and keeps its fragrance for a long time because it contains six fixatives.

2 cups each cedarwood and dried wormwood
1½ cups each dried lavender and dried tansy
¼ cup dried sweet woodruff
1 cup oakmoss
½ cup each dried patchouli, sandalwood, dried southernwood, vetiver root, dried rosemary, whole cloves

1. Powder all ingredients by whirling them in a coffee grinder or spice mill. Mix well.
2. Age for 2 to 4 weeks in a glass jar, then make up sachets.

Shoe Bag Sachets

This formula covers up odors that emanate from stinky sneakers. For especially bad problems, use zeolite or baking soda in shoes while waiting for the fragrance blend to age. (Baking soda makes leather brittle, so it's best to keep its use to a minimum.)

> 3 cups natural clay cat box litter
> 3–9 tablespoons essential oil (see below for suggestions)

Mix together the cat box litter and oil. Age in a glass jar for a week.
Use. Fill socks or pantyhose with the scented clay pellets. Close off the ends with rubber bands. Cover the rubber bands with a ribbon or a bit of twine, if you wish. Place in shoes and leave overnight or longer.

PERSONAL FAVORITES

Sweet Mix: Equal parts orange and balsam of Peru essential oils, with a touch of lemon essential oil

Icy Winter Winds: 1 tablespoon peppermint essential oil, 1 teaspoon rosemary essential oil, ½ teaspoon clove essential oil, ½ teaspoon patchouli essential oil, ¼ teaspoon white camphor essential oil (do not use this combination if you are pregnant)

SIMMERING POTPOURRIS

My favorite way to spread the joys of herbal scents throughout our home is by simmering our favorite botanicals. I keep a large pot of potpourri mixture simmering on the back burner of the stove most of the winter, and the fine vapor adds moisture to our dry, heated air while it disseminates fragrances that not only lift our spirits, but also invisibly battle airborne microbes.

If you have favorite dry potpourri mixes loaded with woods, barks, roots, and spices, you may be able to simmer them, although

Simple Sachet Bag

For a 3-inch-square sachet, cut a piece of fabric 4" x 9". Fold the fabric in half crosswise, right sides together. Sew both side seams, taking a ½-inch seam allowance (A). Turn the raw edge under ¼ inch, and then turn under again; stitch along the fold. Turn the bag right side out. Fill about two-thirds full with sachet (B).

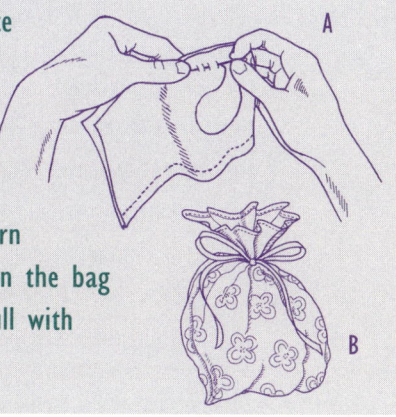

---

the ratios of the ingredients may have to be changed. For instance, the fragrance of dried thyme intensifies when simmered, even overcoming the usually strong, spicy aroma of cloves. Mints, lemon balm, and lemon verbena have ephemeral fragrances that must be replenished frequently. Citrus fruit peels are wonderful, but when their essential oils evaporate, they simply smell like cooked fruit.

Aromatic Air Cleanser Simmering Potpourri

Unlike dried potpourri, simmering potpourri does not need a fixative to blend its scents and make them last longer. Here, however, the fixative calamus adds its own unique fragrance.

  2 cups dried Thuja cedar leaves (arborvitae) and twigs
  1 cup each calamus root, elecampane root, and flowering hyssop tops

Combine all ingredients and mix well.
Use. Use about 1 cup in 4 cups of water, and simmer until the fragrance is gone.
Storage. Store remaining dry mixture in a glass jar in a cool, dark place.

Sinus-Clearing Simmer

Developed as a steam to help clear up bronchial problems, this formula can double as a facial steaming blend if you have oily or troubled skin. You can also infuse it in vinegar for use in cleaning.

> 4 cups dried lavender
> 3 cups dried eucalyptus leaves
> 1 cup each bay leaves, dried grapefruit peel, dried lemon peel, dried rosemary, dried roses, and dried sage
> ½ cup each cinnamon chips, whole allspice, and whole cloves
> 2 tablespoons, plus 1½ teaspoons each whole black peppercorns and whole cardamom pods

Combine all ingredients and toss to mix thoroughly.

Use. Use about 1 cup at a time in 4 cups of simmering water. Add more water and/or herb mix, as needed. When the fragrance is finally exhausted, toss the residue into the compost.

Storage. Store dry mixture in a glass jar in a cool, dark place.

Sleep Pillow Blend

Now that your home is sparkling and smells fantastic, you've earned a night of calm, sweet sleep and wonderful dreams. This dried herb combination makes a pleasant, slightly sweet aromatic fragrance with a calming effect. Relax and enjoy!

> 4½ cups sweet woodruff leaves
> 2 cups lavender flowers
> 1¾ cups rose petals
> 1 cup each of chamomile flowers, jasmine flowers, and oakmoss lichen
> ½ cup each of angelica root chips, calamus root chips or slices, and linden flowers
> 4 tablespoons each of meadowsweet, mugwort leaves, and yarrow flowers
> 2 tablespoons each of anise seed and yellow sandalwood chips

1. Combine all of the dried herbs until well blended, crushing the leaves gently between your fingers to break them up into smaller bits, and place the mixture in a large, covered glass jar.
2. Age the blend in a cool, dark place for 4 weeks, then stuff the herbs into a zippered neckroll pillow case and cover with a heavy quilted case. Tuck this pillow in among your bed pillows or under your neck before you go to sleep each night.

Your Herbal Cleaning Closet

On the following pages are several invaluable charts with information about the ingredients used in many of the housekeeping formulas in the book. Herbal Housekeeping Ingredients describes the many useful additives and bases that are included in the recipes. In addition to information about the appearance and characteristics of each ingredient, the chart tells you how to use it most effectively and where you can purchase it. This is followed by charts listing fixatives and essential oils that enhance and strengthen your cleaning products. We hope you'll find these references handy as you explore this new world of sweet-smelling, effective herbal housekeeping.

Herbal Housekeeping Ingredients

NAME	WHERE TO PURCHASE	PHYSICAL APPEARANCE
Baking soda (sodium bicarbonate)	Grocery store (Arm and Hammer)	Soft, white crystalline powder
Beeswax	Local beekeeper (for best price)	Soft, honey-scented wax produced by bees; naturally golden in color, but bleached for cosmetic products
Bentonite (sodium bentonite)	Some health food stores	Clay, formed by the decomposition of volcanic ash
Borax (sodium tetraborate decahydrate)	Grocery store (Mule Team)	White powdery mineral
Boric acid	Pharmacy, home center, hardware store (in the pesticide department)	Odorless white powder, created by adding sulfuric or hydrochloric acid to borax solution
Bran	Health food store	Outer, fibrous coating of cereal grains
Carnauba wax	Woodworking supplier	Very hard wax derived from the leaves of the Brazilian wax palm tree
Castile bar and liquid soaps	Health food store, mail-order supplier (Dr. Bronner's Liquid Castile and Bar Soaps, Kiss My Face, Baby Liquid Castile)	Bar or liquid soap
Chalk (calcium carbonate)	Grocery store (Bon Ami)	White powdery mineral derived from limestone
Citric acid	Grocery store, mail-order supplier	White crystalline powder made from lemon, lime, or pineapple juice by mold fermentation
Citrus solvent	Health food store, mail-order supplier (Citra-Solv)	Translucent orange liquid
Clay-based cat box litter	Grocery store, pet supply store	Absorbent clay pellets
Cocoa butter	Health food store, pharmacy, mail-order supplier	Fatty substance, solid at room temperature, extracted from cacao beans
Cream of tartar	Grocery store, mail-order supplier	White crystalline powder, a by-product of winemaking
Diatomaceous earth	Garden supply store, swimming pool supplier (Concern)	Powder; the pulverized fossils of small ancient sea plants called diatoms
Fuller's earth	Ceramic or hobby store, home center	Porous clay

CHARACTERISTICS	USES
Abrasive, absorbent, acid neutralizer	Scouring powder, odor neutralizer, stain and spill absorber
Soluble in oils, but not in water, vinegar, glycerin, or alcohol; melting point is about 145°F; flammable	Wax, polish, candles, molds
Not soluble in water, but can absorb several times its volume in liquids	Stain and spill absorber
Soluble in water; moderately toxic	Cleaning and laundry products, insect pest control (microcrystalline residue harms roaches and other crawling insects)
Soluble in water, glycerin, and alcohol	Insect pest control (toxic to roaches)
Keeps well, as it lacks oils; oat bran is lighter in color than wheat bran, so residue shows less	Upholstery spot cleaner
Melting point 185°F; flammable (use double boiler to melt); may cause allergic reaction	Floor wax, furniture polish
Mild, unscented	Laundry detergent, surface cleaner
Only slightly soluble in water, but very soluble in acid solutions; mildly abrasive	Soft scrubber, metal polish
Antioxidant so it serves as a preservative; removes soap scum and mineral deposits	Preservative in many products; scouring powder
Made from citrus, augmented with essential and other oils, and a detergent	Thinner
Unscented	Sachets and other scented products
Pleasant, sweet, light-chocolate scent; melting point of about 92°F	Furniture cream, leather cream
Water-soluble leavening agent	Toilet cleaner, aluminum cleaner, spot remover
Gritty	Household and garden insect pest control
Highly absorptive	Grease remover

Herbal Housekeeping Recipes

Herbal Housekeeping Ingredients (continued)

NAME	WHERE TO PURCHASE	PHYSICAL APPEARANCE
Herbal shampoo	Health food store, mail-order supplier	Liquid
Hydrogen peroxide	Pharmacy, health food store	Clear liquid
Incense charcoals	Religious goods store, mail-order supplier	Small, self-lighting briquettes of carbonized plant material
Jeweler's rouge (iron oxide)	Jewelry, hobby, or craft supply store	Fine reddish brown powder
Jojoba oil	Health food store, mail-order supplier	Wax derived from the seeds of a North American shrub (*Simmondsia californica*); looks like an oil
Lanolin	Pharmacy, mail-order supplier	Refined wool grease; light brown in color
Lifetree's Premium Dishwashing Liquid with Aloe & Calendula	Health food store, mail-order supplier	Liquid detergent
Mineral oil (liquid petrolatum)	Pharmacy	Clear oil distilled from petroleum
Mineral spirits	Paint store, home center	Clear liquid distilled from petroleum
Murphy's Oil Soap	Paint store	Vegetable-based soap made from pine bark; buy the jellylike concentrate
Paraffin wax	Craft or hobby supply store, hardware or grocery store	White wax derived from petroleum
Salt (sodium chloride)	Grocery or health food store (buy noniodized, pickling salt)	White, abrasive crystalline powder
Sodium perborate	Grocery store (as an "all-fabric bleach"), health food store	Odorless white powder
Turpentine	Paint or artist's supply store	Clear, volatile liquid with an oily feel, steam-distilled from the sap of trees (such as the longleaf pine and terebinth)
Vermiculite	Garden center	White, highly porous mineral
Washing soda, or soda ash	Grocery store	White powder
Zeolite	Dasun Company (see page 153)	Naturally occurring mineral found at the sites of active volcanoes

CHARACTERISTICS	USES
Sudsing liquid dissolves dirt and grease	Laundry agent for wool, cashmere, silk, goose down, and other animal fibers
Highly toxic in concentrated form, but available commercially in a 3% solution	Disinfectant; bleach for fabrics of protein origin, such as silk and wool
Used to burn gums, resins, or materials like sweet grass, which must remain in touch with a smoldering source of flame to burn	Incense
Soluble in acids	Metal polish
Does not go rancid	Wax, polish, wood finish
Strong odor	Leather restorer
Sudsing liquid dissolves dirt and grease	Stain pretreatment, hand-washing laundry product
Does not go rancid	Wax, polish, wood finish
Flammable	Paint thinner, floor wax
Pleasant fragrance	Surface cleaner, especially for painted and varnished wood
Soluble in turpentine, warm alcohol, and olive oil; melting point of about 140°F; flammable (use a double boiler to melt); less expensive than beeswax	Often mixed with beeswax in formulas and candles
Water soluble	Scouring powder
A natural bleach, releases oxygen when it decomposes in water	Bleach, disinfectant
Fresh, pungent, in-your-face aroma	Wood finish, floor and furniture wax, oil paint thinner
Insoluble except in hot acids	Container soil mixture
Soluble in water but not in alcohol; wear rubber gloves as it can irritate skin; moderately toxic	Laundry aid, surface cleaner, disinfectant
Has a negative charge (constantly attracts ions); can be solarized and used again	Odor and pollutant absorbant

Herbal Housekeeping Recipes

Essential Oils for Housekeeping

ESSENTIAL OIL	CHARACTERISTICS AND USES	SAFETY LEVEL	PRICE
Anise	Sweet scent; relaxes and calms; promotes sleep; alleviates stress; disinfects	Safe to 2.5% dilution; higher dilution may cause skin irritation.	$$
Camphor, white	Repels insects and prevents hatching of larvae; counters depression	Least toxic of various forms of camphor; nonirritating and non-sensitizing; can cause convulsions; should be avoided by pregnant women and epileptics not on medication.	$
Cedarwood, red	Antiseptic; repels moths and insects; fixative	Nonirritating to skin.	$$
Cinnamon leaf	Warm, spicy fragrance, more medicinal than edible; cleans and disinfects	Safe to 10% dilution.	$$
Citronella	Repels mosquitoes	The citronellal it contains may be mildly irritating to the skin.	$
Clove bud	Antibacterial, antiparasitical, and antifungal; stimulates, energizes, and warms	Wear gloves and use it in low dilutions, as it can irritate the skin. Undiluted clove bud oil is strong enough to melt some plastics and to damage the surface of some metals, so use even diluted clove bud oil with caution, and test on a small area first.	$$$
Eucalyptus	Antibacterial (effective against staph, strep, pneumonia, and viruses); a 2% dilution, sprayed into the air, will kill 70 percent of airborne staph; antifungal	Nonirritating to skin.	$$
Fir	Pinelike fragrance; energizes, focuses, and uplifts	Use oil within 6 months to avoid skin irritation.	$$
Grapefruit	Citrus scent; stimulates pain relief (thus good for cleaning sickrooms)	Makes skin slightly sensitive to sunlight, so wear gloves. Avoid exposure to sun if 4% solution gets on skin.	$$

Key: $ = about $10–15 for 4 ounces
$$ = about $15–20 for 4 ounces
$$$ = about $20–25 for 4 ounces

Essential Oils for Housekeeping (continued)

ESSENTIAL OIL	CHARACTERISTICS AND USES	SAFETY LEVEL	PRICE
Lavender	Antibacterial, antiviral, and antifungal; calms, enhances immune system	Very safe.	$$$
Lemon	Antiviral and antibacterial (including staph, strep, and pneumonia); fresh, clean scent soothes and uplifts; negative charge attracts dust	Wear gloves. If dilution higher than 2% gets on skin, avoid sunlight for 12 hours.	$
Lemongrass	Disinfects; soothes; may protect against scabies and ringworm	Nonirritating, except to damaged skin.	$$
Lime	Refreshes, energizes, and uplifts	Causes skin to be sensitive to sun. Wear gloves. If dilution higher than 0.7% gets on skin, avoid sunlight for 12 hours.	$$
Orange, sweet	Antiviral, antibacterial, and antidepressant; enhances immune system; repels fleas	Very safe. Does not cause skin sensitivity to sun.	$
Peppermint	Antiviral, antiparasitical, and antibacterial; stimulates and energizes	Avoid exposure if you suffer from cardiac fibrillation.	$$
Pine	Antibacterial and antiviral; invigorates, energizes, and uplifts; stimulates immune system	Use within 6 months to avoid skin irritation.	$$
Rosemary	Antibacterial; activates the brain, memory, and energy; dissolves grease; repels insects (high camphor content)	Pregnant women and epileptics not on medication should avoid rosemary oil.	$$$
Rosewood	Antibacterial; rose geranium fragrance; induces tranquillity	Very safe.	$$$
Spearmint	Antidepressant, antiseptic	Safer than peppermint, since it lacks menthol and pulegone.	$$
Tangerine	Antiviral, antibacterial, and antidepressant; enhances immune system; repels fleas	Very safe.	$
Tea tree	Antibacterial, antiviral, antifungal, and antiseptic; enhances immune system	Very safe.	$$$

Fixatives for Housekeeping

COMMON NAME	BOTANICAL NAME	FORMS USED
Ambrette, Musk	*Hibiscus abelmoschus, H. moscheutos*	Seed, essential oil
Angelica	*Angelica archangelica*	Root, essential oil
Balsam of Peru	*Myroxylon pereirae*	Essential oil
Balsam of tolu	*Myroxylon balsamum*	Essential oil
Benzoin	*Styrax* species (especially *S. benzoin*)	Gum (powdered), absolute
Calamus	*Acorus americanus*	Root
Cedarwood	*Juniperus virginiana*	Wood chips, essential oil
Clary sage	*Salvia sclarea*	Flowers, buds, leaves, essential oil
Copaiba balsam	*Copaifera langsdorffii* (syn. *Copaiba officinalis*)	Gum
Copal, Amber	*Buresera fugaroides*	Gum
Deer's tongue	*Trilisa odoratissima*	Leaves
Frankincense	*Boswellia carterii*	Gum, in "tears" (droplets) or powdered, absolute
Galbanum	*Ferula galbaniflua*	Resin
Myrrh	*Commiphora myrrha*	Resin, absolute
Oakmoss lichen	*Evernia prunastri*	Lichen (whole or powdered), absolute

CHARACTERISTICS AND USES	SAFETY TIPS
Sweet, sensual, earthy musklike scent	Essential oil is very safe for housekeeping uses.
Use with fruity, sweet, herbal, or woody fragrances	The essential oil causes phototoxic reactions (sunburn and blotchy skin).
Extremely sweet, vanilla-like fragrance; blends nicely with citrus fragrances; useful for taking the bitter, drying edge off other scents	May be a skin irritant.
Similar to balsam of Peru; combined with oil and used to treat raw wood, makes a hard, deliciously scented finish	May be a skin irritant.
Pleasantly scented white gum; use the powder in floral sachets; use the absolute in other fragrance products	May be a skin irritant; don't use the toxic tincture of benzoin (a different product altogether) as a fixative.
Aromatic, calming, somewhat medicinal fragrance	Essential oil is potentially carcinogenic.
Mellows with age; low, deep, grounding fragrance	Safe for housekeeping uses.
Relaxing, musklike, sweaty fragrance that improves with age	Essential oil contains estrogen-like substances, and should be avoided by those with breast cysts or cancer.
Fragrance similar to myrrh; oil used in soaps and perfumes	Safe for housekeeping uses.
Pleasant, though not as sweet or strong as frankincense; can be burned as an incense or fumigant	Safe for housekeeping uses.
Strongly sweet and somewhat fruity scent	Safe for housekeeping uses.
Sweet, uplifting, powerful but not coercive; burn as incense or incorporate the tears or powdered gum into sachets, and potpourris	Safe for housekeeping uses.
Sharp, strong, green, woody, somewhat spicy aroma	Safe for housekeeping uses.
Pungent and aromatic; burn as incense, incorporate in sachets and potpourris; extract resin in alcohol	Safe for housekeeping uses.
Sweet fragrance; blends well with woody or haylike scents (such as sweet woodruff); insect repellent	May cause skin irritation; contains toxic thujones; avoid during pregnancy.

Herbal Housekeeping Recipes

Fixatives for Housekeeping (continued)

COMMON NAME	BOTANICAL NAME	FORMS USED
Orrisroot	*Iris germanica* var. *florentina*	Root, absolute
Patchouli	*Pogostemon cablin*	Leaves, essential oil
Queen Anne's lace	*Daucus carota*	Seed, essential oil (sold as "carrot seed oil")
Red sandalwood	*Pterocarpus santalinus*	Wood
Storax	*Styrax officinalis*	Resin
Sweet clover, Melilot	*Melilotus officinalis*	Flowers, buds, leaves
Sweet grass	*Hierochloe odorata*	Grass blades
Sweet woodruff	*Galium odoratum*	Leaves
Tonka	*Dipteryx odorata*	Beans
Vanilla grass	*Anthoxanthum odoratum*	Grass blades
Vetiver	*Vetiveria zizanioides*	Root, essential oil
Wild gingerroot, Canada snakeroot	*Asarum canadense*	Root
Yellow sandalwood	*Santalum album*	Wood, essential oil

CHARACTERISTICS AND USES	SAFETY TIPS
Sweet violet scent; excellent with other floral fragrances	Wear gloves when handling root, as it often causes skin irritation; use only in potpourris and sachets.
Rich, earthy scent when fresh; essential oil is very sharp and pungent; mellows after about 15 years	Safe for housekeeping uses.
Spicy, aromatic, and a bit fruity; essential oil is stronger, very pungent	Safe for housekeeping uses.
Woody; drier, much less sweet balsamic scent than yellow sandalwood; striking color	Safe for housekeeping uses.
Pleasant, vanilla scent	Possibly a skin irritant.
Newmown-hay, vanilla-like scent increases upon fermentation and drying	Safe for housekeeping uses.
Develops a much stronger, sweeter aroma when dry	Safe for housekeeping uses.
Light, pleasant, newmown-hay fragrance, increases when dry	Safe for housekeeping uses.
Sweet, newmown-hay fragrance; repels pests; loses sweetness with age	Safe for housekeeping uses. Keep beans from small children.
Newmown-hay, vanilla-like fragrance; grows in a mound shape, and thus more controllable in the garden than is sweet grass	Safe for housekeeping uses.
Dominant, strong, earthy, woodsy fragrance; use sparingly and then evaluate	Safe for housekeeping uses.
Spicy, earthy aroma with a skunky undertone; similar to but sweeter than valerian	Don't use the essential oil, which is carcinogenic to rodents, and so potentially dangerous to humans.
One of my favorites; sweet, rich, warm, soothing, and uplifting; very complementary to many other fragrance types	Safe as chipped wood, powder, or essential oil.

Herbal Housekeeping Recipes

CHAPTER 5

GROWING, PRESERVING, AND *Using Herbs*

If I had space for only the tiniest garden, herbs are the plants I would choose to grow. There's something sacred and timeless about herbs. Because the parsley, sage, rosemary, and thyme we grow today are descendants of the very plants the ancient Greeks and Romans used, just breathing their fragrance makes me feel connected to countless generations who have shared the same simple delight. Along with this link to the past, herbs provide many opportunities to take charge of life, create pleasures, and satisfy personal needs. The pungent flavor of fresh basil, the soothing comfort of a cup of chamomile tea, and the physical delight of digging in the earth can be grounding and strengthening. May the generosity of the good earth and the green growing plants fill your heart as well.

Where to Grow Herbs

Happily, herbs are among the easiest plants to grow. Given enough sunlight and good drainage, herbs will grow in almost any type of soil, and most can withstand long periods of drought. And because of their aromatic nature, most herbs seem to repel destructive insects and hungry wildlife, too.

If your site is boggy or densely shaded, give container growing a try. (For advice about growing herbs in containers, see page 141.) Because planters heat up and drain faster than in-ground plantings, many herbs that sulk in cool, damp conditions will grow happily in pots. And a few herbs actually prefer partial shade over full sun. These include angelica, chervil, cilantro, comfrey, lemon balm, mints, sweet cicely, sweet woodruff, and violets. A few sun-preferring herbs will also adapt to partial shade, especially once the weather warms up. Try situating borage, burnet, dill, fennel, hyssop, parsley, and sage in light shade.

You don't need a separate garden for your herbs. Although most herbs aren't typically grown for their blossoms, most have attractive shapes and foliage, so they combine beautifully with flowering plants and shrubs. Tuck annual herbs like basil, dill, and marjoram into flower

Ideal Site for an Herb Garden

Although herbs are remarkably resilient and adaptable, you will have the greatest success with most herbs if you give them a spot with the following conditions:

- Full sun at least 6 hours a day
- Well-drained (no long-lasting puddles when it rains)
- Conveniently located to the hose and the kitchen
- Limited competition from large trees that draw water and nutrients
- Protected from marauding pets and children's play areas
- Located away from underground utility lines and the septic tank or other water and sewer lines
- Relatively flat site

beds and vegetable gardens. Perennial herbs like sage, lovage, and thyme will be right at home in established flower beds, and they're good partners for asparagus and rhubarb in a perennial vegetable patch.

Laying the Groundwork

Creating a design is the first step in establishing a new garden site. Gather ideas from other gardens and gardening books and magazines. Rectangles and squares are usually the easiest shapes to work with, but if the site or your heart begs for something different, follow your inspiration. I never plant in straight lines, even though my artistic notions usually create more challenging spaces to maintain.

To preview your garden layout, outline the perimeter with a hose or rope. Spread newspaper to mark the bed. Stand back and imagine what you'd like to plant where. Before going inside, mark the bed with stakes and sketch your ideas on paper. Later, spend time plotting herb placement, taking into consideration ultimate size, shape, and color, as well as seasonal factors like early- and late-season crops.

Edible Knot Gardens

Traditionally worked in perennial herbs like lavender and germander, knot gardens are stunning, but they can be an expensive and time-consuming investment. Here's a cheaper option, especially if you start plants from seed: Use basils! For a formal look, select a compact basil such as basil 'Finissimo Verde' or 'Spicy Globe'. Make a color splash and interplant 'Dark Opal' basil with a green-leafed form. A bonus beyond the aesthetic appeal of this garden: You can eat the results!

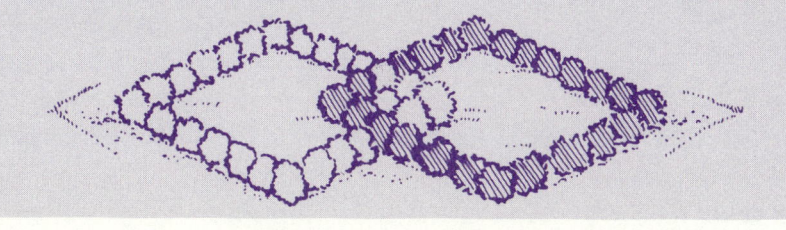

Growing, Preserving, and Using Herbs

SALAD GARDEN

Create a complete salad garden using recycled wooden crates, or build your own boxes from wood scraps. For longer life, treat the wood with boiled linseed oil. (Do not use pressure-treated wood, as the chemicals that kill rot, which are living organisms, can also kill plants.) Lining the wood with heavy-duty plastic also helps retard rot. Be sure to punch drainage holes in the plastic. If you take both of these preventive measures, your salad garden containers should hold up for five to seven years. I like to intermingle edible flowers (calendula and Johnny-jump-ups) and greens, such as arugula and several varieties of lettuce, with salad herbs in this decorative mini-garden. Follow the advice on growing herbs in containers, beginning on page 141.

1. Nasturtium *(Tropaeolum majus)*
2. Arugula *(Eruca sativa)*
3. Lettuce
4. Bronze fennel *(Foeniculum vulgare 'Bronze')*
5. Calendula *(Calendula officinalis)*
6. Lettuce-leaf basil *(Ocimum basilicum 'Crispum')*
7. Dill *(Anethum graveolens)*
8. Garlic chives *(Allium tuberosum)*
9. Lemon basil *(Ocimum basilicum 'Citriodorum')*
10. Johnny-jump-ups *(Viola tricolor)*
11. Sweet marjoram *(Origanum majorana)*
12. Summer savory *(Satureja hortensis)*
13. Lemon thyme *(Thymus serpyllum 'Citriodorus')*
14. Italian parsley *(Petroselinum crispum* var. *neapolitanum)*
15. Chives *(Allium schoenoprasum)*

SALSA GARDEN

Here's enough spicy heat to keep salsa lovers happy all summer! For tomato-based dips that don't drip, choose meaty, small-fruited tomato varieties such as red 'Roma' and 'Juliet', and yellow 'Wonder Light' and 'Yellow Bell'. Other colorful salsa tomatoes include medium-size golden types like 'Djena Lee' and 'Golden Jubilee'; 'Eva Purple' is a variety with beautiful pink-purple fruit. Tomatillos are 1- to 2-inch green fruits that grow within a thin husk. They like the same treatment you'd give tomatoes, including sun and heat; they don't need staking. Be sure to plant only one quillquina: this plant can grow 4 to 5 feet tall. By the way, please *do* eat the flowers in this design. Mexican roses are kissing cousins to the potherb purslane *(Portulaca oleracea)*. Both flowers and leaves are edible.

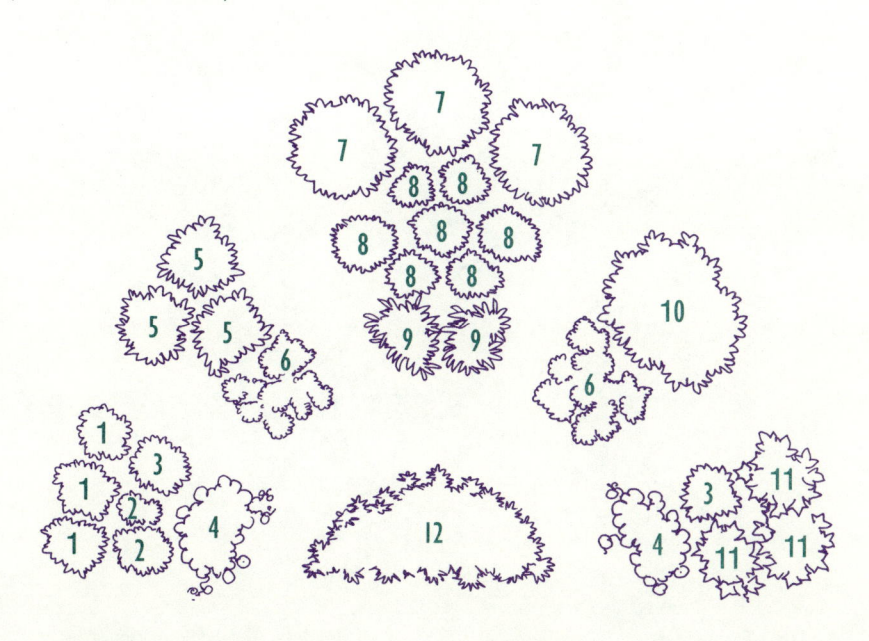

1. Tomatillos
2. Cinnamon basil *(Ocimum basilicum 'Cinnamon')*
3. Jalapeño peppers
4. Nasturtiums *(Tropaeolum majus)*
5. Bell pepper
6. Cilantro *(Coriandrum sativum)*
7. Tomatoes
8. Basil *(Ocimum basilicum)*
9. Calendula *(Calendula officinalis)*
10. Quillquina *(Porophyllum ruderale)*
11. Cucumbers
12. Mexican roses *(Portulaca grandiflora)*

Growing, Preserving, and Using Herbs

SPAGHETTI OR PIZZA GARDEN

Here's a summer garden loaded with the makings for pasta sauces and pizza toppings. For thick sauces, choose meaty small and medium-size tomatoes (see page 135 for variety names). 'Anaheim' and 'Ancho' are flavorful pepper varieties; jalapeños offer comfortable heat. For a sweeter pepper, try 'Sweet Chocolate'. And for heat lovers, habañero peppers (especially 'Red Savina') hit the top of the Scovill heat-rating scale for fire! For healthy green pizza toppings, grow a patch of mixed greens, such as chard, arugula, and chicory. Use nasturtium and calendula petals as colorful, decorative accents when you serve.

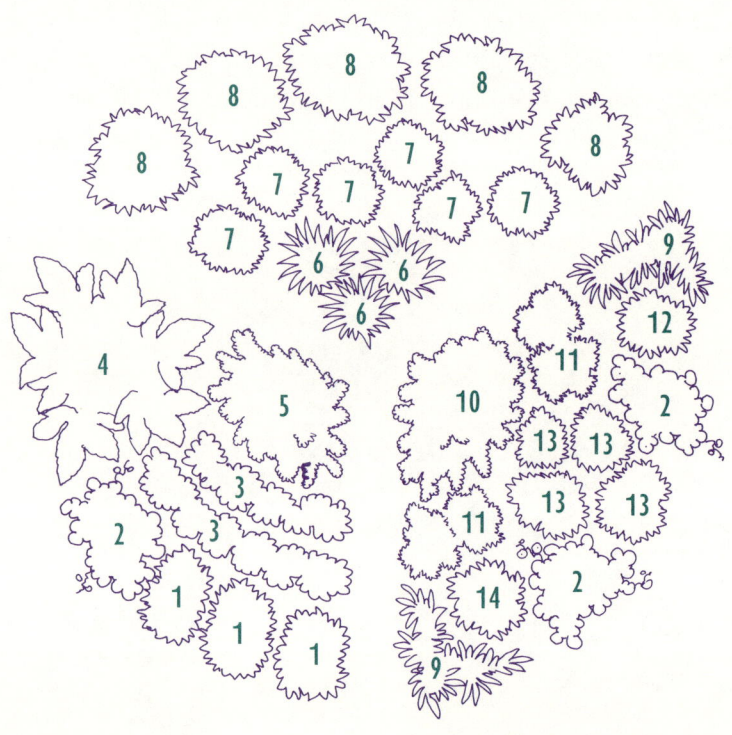

1. Jalapeño peppers
2. Nasturtiums *(Tropaeolum majus)*
3. Mixed greens
4. Zucchini
5. Oregano *(Origanum vulgare)*
6. Garlic chives *(Allium tuberosum)*
7. Basil *(Ocimum basilicum* 'Genovese')
8. Tomatoes
9. Calendula *(Calendula officinalis)*
10. Sweet marjoram *(Origanum majorana)*
11. Italian parsley *(Petroselinum crispum var. neapolitanum)*
12. Anaheim pepper
13. Bell pepper
14. Ancho pepper

Household Herbs

A Seed-Saver's Herb Garden

Seed saving is a wonderful way to furnish your own garden, help other gardeners, and ensure seeds for future generations. Let's say you have several wonderful plants of lemon basil. In late summer, allow some of the plants to flower, then wither until dark stalks develop where the flowers were. Before the frost comes, clip off the entire seed stalk, and place it in a paper bag, which will catch any seeds that might fall out.

When you have time, spread some white paper on a work table and empty the stalks on the paper. You'll probably see some tiny black seeds among the brown chaff. Pick those out and place them in a paper envelope. To find the remaining seeds, strip the seed capsules from the flower stalks and place them in a wire mesh strainer. Rub the plant material against the mesh to release more seeds. If there's a lot of chaff mixed in with the seeds, blow lightly to dispel the debris. Once you've gathered all the seeds, close the envelope and label it with the type of seed and the year harvested. Most seeds will remain viable for three to five years if stored in a cool, dry place, but dill, cilantro, fennel, and other herbs in the carrot family are best planted within a year after harvesting.

Lemon basil seed stalk

Remove chaff by pressing plant material against strainer.

In addition to sharing seeds within your local community, consider joining the Seed Savers Exchange, a national nonprofit organization committed to preserving biodiversity. SSE focuses on vegetables, fruits, and grains, whereas a sister network, the Flower and Herb Exchange, is devoted exclusively to flowers and herbs. (See Herbal Resources for address.)

Digging In

Once you've determined where to plant, you can prepare the soil. My favorite method requires very little digging. Begin by mowing the site, using the lowest setting on the mower. (If your soil is clay, till the soil after mowing.) To suffocate the grass, spread newspaper at least eight pages thick over the mowed area. Keep the newspaper in place and prevent it from wicking moisture from the soil by soaking it with water, then covering it with at least 2 inches of compost, topsoil, or a good soil mix. Add a balanced organic fertilizer at the rate listed on the package. Add lime only if a soil test indicates that you need it. Rake the bed smooth, then sprinkle it with water until it's evenly moist. When the weather is right, set in your plants, cutting right through the newspaper with a trowel to make the planting holes. This method works even better if the site is prepared the autumn previous to spring planting.

If you want good soil in a hurry, consider purchasing a load of topsoil and spreading it on top of the newspaper to a depth of 6 to 8 inches. Be sure to investigate the quality of the soil before it's dumped in your yard. I buy a product that's half composted leaves and half topsoil. Having soil that's easy to dig in makes every garden activity a breeze.

Use a trowel to cut through soil, layers of newspaper, and sod.

Seeds and Transplants

Once you've created a place to plant, select five herbs you already know you like and one or two you'd like to learn about. For many herbs, one plant of each variety is enough for the average family, but you may want two or three plants of frequently used annual herbs, such as basil, dill, and cilantro. If you plan to make lots of pesto or brew herb vinegars, you'll need at least a dozen plants of each.

When choosing herbs and planning where you will make homes for them, it's helpful to understand that plants have different types of life cycles.

Hardy annuals. Annuals are plants that complete their growth cycle (grow, flower, set seed, and die) in one growing season. Some favorite hardy annual herbs are borage, calendula, chervil, cilantro, and dill. Of these, chervil, cilantro, and dill grow best from seed sown at the cooler ends of the growing season. To get a head start, sow them in late fall where you want plants to grow; they'll sprout the following spring. Or, sow them several weeks before the last frost in the spring. Either way you'll be able to harvest them until summer heats up.

Warm-weather or tender annuals. Wait until frosts are behind you before planting basils, nasturtiums, and summer savory. It's easy to start these annuals from seed in warm soil if you remember to keep the area moist until plants emerge, or purchase one or two transplants.

Perennials. Perennials can be divided into two groups: hardy perennials, like lavender, mint, sage, and thyme, which tolerate freezing conditions; and tender perennials, such as bay, scented-leaf geraniums, lemongrass, rosemary, and lemon verbena, which don't. Consult a garden encyclopedia for advice on the hardiness range of the perennial herbs you'd like to grow. (Hardiness zones indicate the average annual minimum temperatures of various regions of North America. Check with your local nursery to find out your area's hardiness zone.)

Many hardy perennial herbs are easy to grow. For quickest results, start with purchased transplants or cuttings from a friend, as perennials grown from seed often take two seasons to develop into mature plants. Plant hardy perennials in early to late spring, so they will have time to get well established before the weather gets hot.

Unless you live in Zone 9 or 10, it's best to grow tender perennials in pots that can be brought indoors at summer's end. You can sink the pots in the ground, so that you can remove the plant, pot and all, without disturbing its roots, or enjoy it as a container plant on the porch or deck outdoors in summer, and bring it in for winter.

Growing-Season Care

Most in-ground herbs need little care once planted. If Mother Nature doesn't provide, water new transplants every day or two until the rain fills in. Once herbs are off and growing, they aren't likely to require supplemental water unless drought becomes severe. I add seaweed solution to the water (2 tablespoons solution per gallon of water) when I put in new herb plants, but that's typically the extent of any fertilizing program. However, if you have a small garden and harvest regularly, you may want faster growth. In that case, foliar feed every 3 weeks. (See page 143.)

Mulch. Good mulches for herbs are shredded leaves, dried grass clippings, or straw. Do not use heavy wood chips, especially if you are growing lavender or other herbs that dislike acidity. These mulches not only pack down and suffocate roots, but wood chips, as well as pine needles and oak leaves, are also very acidic.

Pruning. Regular trimming keeps growth more tender and sweet. Every 2 weeks, walk through your garden with pruners or scissors in hand, and snip off unwanted buds, trim back leggy growth, and cut off any weak-looking branches. Remove as much as a third of the plant if necessary.

Prune plants regularly, and use clippings in your cooking.

Winter care. In early winter, cover hardy perennials like lavender, sage, and thyme with a light mulch. The mulch keeps the soil from alternately freezing and thawing, which is the biggest cause of winterkill where snow cover is not reliable. Evergreen branches placed loosely around the base of the plants are perfect for this purpose. (Remember to remove the branches in the spring, so that they don't add acidity to the soil.) If you live in an area where you can count on a deep snow cover, there's no need to mulch, because nature's winter blanket will do the job.

The Potted Herb

Do you have problem soil, no time to prepare soil, too much shade, or no garden soil at all? If you answered yes to any of these questions, container gardening may be the answer for you. Most herbs make ideal container plants, and pots can be located close to the house and situated so that little bending is required.

MATERIAL MATTERS

Keeping your plants moist is the primary challenge of container gardening. Larger containers need less frequent watering, so you can save yourself time by planting several plants in one large container. Determine what size container to use by the number of plants: Four transplants from 4-inch pots fit well in a 10-inch container. Wooden containers, such as half-whiskey barrels, retain moisture and "breathe," so soil stays cooler during hot spells. Airtight plastic pots also retain moisture, but black plastic absorbs heat from the sun and can virtually bake plants. Clay pots are so porous that moisture quickly wicks away.

Drill plenty of holes in the bottom of all containers for drainage. To improve drainage further and to protect containers and the surface where they sit from rot, place them on bricks or blocks. Beyond these considerations, the choice of containers depends mostly on aesthetics and cost. Besides half-whiskey barrels, I also like to recycle found objects, such as dresser drawers, old wagons, and wooden crates.

Herbs by the Bushel

Bushel baskets are another inexpensive option. Simply line a basket with a plastic trash bag, slash a few holes in the plastic for drainage, and fill it with a good soil mix (see page 142). Placed on bricks, these gardens-to-go — complete with handles — will last all season.

SOIL FOR CONTAINERS

It takes a lot of soil mix to fill large containers, but you don't have to use 100 percent soil. Fill the bottom half of deep containers like half-whiskey barrels with twigs, leaves, or pinecones. Or, use Styrofoam peanuts or aluminum soda cans turned upside down, which have the added advantage of making large containers lighter and therefore easier to move around. Don't fill containers with garden soil; it's just too heavy. A good recipe for a container mix for herbs is equal parts purchased potting soil, sand, and compost. For best results, add granulated organic fertilizer according to package recommendations.

WATER WISELY

Containers dry out much more quickly than in-ground plantings do. Most planters need watering at least every other day during hot summer months. Be sure to place saucers underneath pots to hold extra water, but remember to empty them when there's a rainy spell so the plants don't get waterlogged. Mulching the soil in containers also helps. I use a 2-inch layer of shredded leaves with good success.

Automated Watering

If you will be away frequently and have no one to water in your absence, consider investing in an automatic irrigation system, with spigots that deliver water to each container on a schedule you can program.

- vinyl tubing
- hose
- dripper

FEEDING POTTED HERBS

Herbs planted in the garden generally need very little fertilizer, but life in containers is different. Every time you water, liquid leaches through the container and flushes out water-soluble nutrients as it goes. Every 3 to 4 weeks, I feed all my container plants with a seaweed solution applied to their leaves, using 1 tablespoon seaweed solution per gallon of water in a pump-type sprayer. Called foliar feeding, this is a great supplemental feeding technique, as plants can absorb nutrients much faster through their leaves than through their roots. For best results, foliar feed in the early morning or early evening when the pores of the leaves are open to absorb dew. Use the finest mist setting on the sprayer, and mist both the tops and undersides of the leaves.

All in Good Thyme: An Herb Garden Calendar

Over the years, I've developed a calendar that helps me remember successful garden strategies. This is a rough schedule for my Maryland herb garden, where the average last frost date is May 10–18 and the average first frost is October 10. To adjust for your hardiness zone, compare the dates listed for your zone and subtract or add the number of weeks' difference. To make it easier to create your own herb garden calendar, take photographs throughout the season to document your garden. And keep a written record, so that you can develop a schedule that works for you. Most of all, enjoy being in your garden, drinking in the beauty of life!

January. Use evergreen boughs, such as branches from a discarded Christmas tree, to mulch lavender, sage, thyme, tarragon, and other perennial herbs subject to frost heave. Harvest pine needles for tea (see page 62). Order seed catalogs, read garden books and magazines, take lots of herbal baths, and dream about your garden.

February. Bring dream gardens to earth on paper. Order seeds and other materials. Host an herb seed swap and sample herbal teas. Repair garden tools. Make sure mulch stays in place. Begin pruning evergreen herbs (lavender, sage, thyme) on mild days. Harvest chickweed, garlic mustard, and wintercress. If your soil is acidic, spread lime over receding snow.

March. Rake mulch from beds and sow seeds of hardy annual herbs, like calendula, chervil, cilantro, dill, nigella, and poppies. Harvest early spring potherbs like dandelions and violets. Listen for those first signs of spring: spring peepers, returning geese, and robins.

April. Divide perennial herbs. Take cuttings. Plant new perennials. If you've started plants indoors, transplant hardy annual seedlings. Sow basil, nasturtium, and savory seeds indoors. Finish pruning herbs. Prepare any new garden areas when the soil warms. Renew established gardens with compost and leaf mold. Dye Easter eggs with natural dyes (see page 27). Harvest dandelions, nettles, and other spring wildings. Make a fresh batch of potting soil.

May. Make May Day baskets brimming with herbs and spring flowers. Begin hardening off indoor plants like bay, scented geraniums, and rosemary, as well as seedlings started indoors. Complete preparation of garden beds and containers. Plant annuals when the ground is warm and dry enough to cultivate and frost no longer threatens. Mulch garden pathways. Lie in the grass and watch clouds skip across the sky.

June. Add final touches to the garden, keeping transplants well watered. Keep up with the weeds, mulching if necessary. Harvest and preserve early-spring herbs — calendula, chervil, cilantro, red clover blossoms, dandelions, and nettles. Dance in the moonlight on Midsummer Eve. Celebrate the solstice.

July. Keep herbs and flowers trimmed. Plant a second crop of basil and summer savory if these plants have gone to seed. Begin preserving herbs. Watch the butterflies. Nap in the shade.

August. Early in the month, prune summer herbs by one-third to one-half, and foliar feed to encourage new growth. Sow seeds of hardy annuals (calendula, chervil, cilantro, dill, parsley) and biennials (angelica, caraway), and sow a new crop of salad greens. Take cuttings of basils and scented geraniums for indoor plants. If tender perennials aren't potted, dig them up, cut them back, and keep them in partial shade until bringing indoors before the first frost. Make and freeze pesto. Make herb vinegars. Begin drying herbs. Say good-bye to the hummingbirds. Watch the shadows lengthen.

September. Plant saffron crocus and garlic. Last call for freezing basil. Harvest remaining summer herbs before the first frost. Bring tender perennials indoors. Save seeds. Make Rosemary-Goldenrod Jelly (page 18), herb mustards, herb butters, and other pantry staples. Watch for a new crop of chickweed, dandelions, and nettles.

October. Clean up the garden, clipping off dead foliage at ground level and composting it. Prepare new garden beds. Mulch leaves. Carve pumpkins. Make dried wreaths. Wave to the geese.

November. Finish any remaining garden cleanup. Make notes for next year while you can remember! Give thanks for the bounty of the earth.

December. Prepare holiday gifts. Celebrate the winter solstice!

HERBS ANYTHYME: THE INDOOR HERB GARDEN

Most herbs need strong sunlight to thrive and thus are challenging houseplants, especially during the dark days of winter. But you can enjoy many fresh herbs, and overwinter others, with little extra effort.

In early fall, I gather potted bay, scented geranium, and rosemary plants and set them on an outdoor porch so they'll get accustomed to less light. When frost threatens, I put the rosemaries and as many other plants as I can fit in the sunniest windows in the house. I water the plants twice a week, adding seaweed solution to the water to make life indoors bearable. I also mist the plants once or twice a week to keep up the humidity. Cooler temperatures (55 to 65°F) are ideal. The plants I don't have room for go down to the basement, where it's cool. Because there's not enough light for the plants to flourish, I encourage them to become semi-dormant by watering them only about once every three weeks.

Mist indoor plants weekly.

Growing, Preserving, and Using Herbs

In late March or early April, I trim all the plants, including those that are semi-dormant, repot those whose roots are cramped and need bigger pots, add compost to the pots, and put them in a sheltered spot outdoors when frost is no longer likely. Once weather is dependably mild, I gradually accustom them to outdoor sunlight.

Using this method, scented geraniums grow well for two or three seasons, and rosemary for 4 or 5 years. The bay just keeps going, and the biggest problem I face with it is moving such a large plant!

SUMMER HERBS IN DEEPEST WINTER
If you want to grow summer herbs indoors for more than occasional winter use, you'll find that even your sunniest window doesn't provide enough light for robust growth. For successful indoor herb growing, invest in fluorescent light fixtures. Regular shop lights that hold four tubes provide enough growing area for most families. A mixture of cool white and warm white tubes works well. Hang the light fixture so that you can adjust its height. Position the lights so they are only 6 to 8 inches above plants. (You'll need to raise them as plants grow.) Buy a timer that will turn the lights on and off automatically, and set it for 16 hours on and 8 hours off. This setup is good for starting seeds.

HARVESTING AND STORING HERBS

When is the best time to harvest herbs? The short answer is: Whenever you need them! But if you can wait, or you're harvesting a large number of herbs for storage, the ideal time is just after the morning dew has evaporated or when it cools off in the evening. New gardeners are often timid about cutting herbs, but regular harvesting actually encourages growth. You can vigorously cut back growing plants by one-third to two-thirds of their height without stunting growth. Harvest all annuals completely before the first frost.

Cutting tools. Invest in at least one pair of sharp culinary scissors. They make fast work of cutting both woody and tender stalks without straining your wrists or crushing plants. For clipping tiny chamomile flower heads or tender dill fronds, a pair of small "blossom-size" scissors are ideal. Both pairs are useful for mincing herbs in the kitchen as well.

Harvest basket. Treat yourself to a roomy basket to gather herbs. Line the basket with a pretty tea towel if you like. A flat-bottomed basket will accommodate a few berry baskets to separate herbs, or a plastic container of water to refresh stems if you'll be out in the sun for a while. You can also make layers of different herbs, using damp tea towels to separate them.

THE WHEN AND HOW OF HARVESTING

Leaves. Begin clipping the tender tops when plants are 3 inches tall. On upright, branching plants like basil and rosemary, cut just above a node, which is the spin-off point for new growth. As the plants bush out, trim the branching stems in the same manner (see illustration, page 140). For sprawling plants like marjoram and thyme, gather a few sprigs between your fingers and snip them en masse. For clump-forming plants like chives, dill, and parsley, clip off a few stalks at ground level.

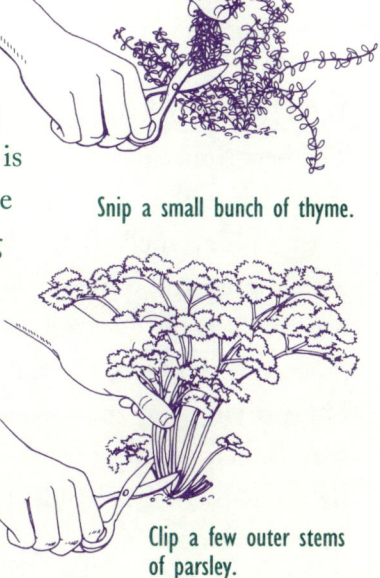

Snip a small bunch of thyme.

Clip a few outer stems of parsley.

Flowers. Harvest flowers when they first open or a little earlier, that is, when the bud just begins to show color. Remove flowers with enough stem to place in water, or just above the next blossom in line to bloom.

Seeds. Cut seed heads as they begin to turn brown but before they shatter (that point at which the seeds fall out of the seedpods). Because seeds ripen unevenly, it's usually safer to finish drying them by hanging the seed heads upside down in a brown paper bag tied off at the top. Be sure to punch a few holes in the sides of the bag to allow for air circulation.

Growing, Preserving, and Using Herbs **147**

CARE OF THE HARVEST

There's no need to wash herbs unless they are visibly dirty. Store herbs for short-term use in a glass of water. First, crush their stems slightly with a wooden spoon. If you're keeping them for more than a day or two, place the glass in a plastic bag, close with a twist tie, and refrigerate. Or wrap cuttings in a damp towel and enclose them in a plastic bag. Close the bag only loosely. Check herbs every other day and remoisten the towel if necessary.

Place herb stems in a glass of water, and store in a plastic bag.

DRYING HERBS FOR WINTER USE

The best time to harvest leafy herbs is just before full flowering, when they're in their prime. Select a sunny day during a dry spell. If the herbs are dirty, rinse them with the hose the night before, so you won't need to wet them again. As soon as possible after harvesting, proceed with one of the following drying methods:

Hang drying. Lay stalks on a counter and sort them by size. Bunch together three to five stem ends and tie tightly with rubber bands, twist ties, or damp twine. (Damp twine shrinks slightly when dry, creating a tighter knot.) If you use twine, cut a piece about 18 inches long, and tie a bunch of herbs on each end. Hang the herbs in an area with good air circulation but out of direct sunlight, which causes fading. String a clothesline in a vacant space or use a clothes-drying rack, and hang bunches of herbs with clothespins. If you don't have a suitable space that's out of direct sunlight, bunch the herbs in paper bags with the stem ends coming out of the top of the bag. Punch several holes in the bag to allow for air circulation. Remember, you have to let out the moisture!

Tie an herb bundle to each end of a piece of twine.

Screen drying. Place a screen on wood blocks, and lay herbs in a single layer on the screen. You can continue stacking wood blocks

> ### Dried Herbs Fresh from the Fridge
>
> Herbs with a lot of water in their leaves, such as basil, dill, and parsley, lose flavor when hang-dried. Here's a better way to preserve them: If you've rinsed your herbs, gently pat them dry with a clean towel and let them air until no moisture is left on the leaves. Place several stems in a single layer in a brown paper bag. Place the bag in a frost-free refrigerator and tape to the side. Within a week, the herbs will be dried, and you can store as for other dried herbs. The defrosting mechanism, which is designed to remove moist air from the refrigerator, draws the moisture from the herbs. Plus, there's no light to discolor the leaves, and the cool temperature preserves flavor.

and additional screens on top to save space while accomodating more herbs.

Mechanical dryers. Follow the manufacturer's instructions for drying herbs with a food dehydrator or microwave.

"Hot box." On a hot, sunny morning, line the seats and floor of your car with newspaper. Lay herbs in a single layer on the paper and then cover with another layer of paper so that the herbs don't fade. Open the windows a bit to allow moisture to escape. By the end of the day, herbs should be ready to store.

STORING DRIED HERBS

Although it's pleasant to see herbs hanging from the kitchen ceiling, this exposure to moisture in the air quickly degrades their flavor. Reserve some bunches for decoration if you like, but store those you'll cook with as soon as the leaves are crackly dry. Unless you live in an arid climate, it's wise to "finish off" hang-dried herbs with a brief stint in the oven. Strip the leaves from the stems, taking care not to crumble the leaves more than necessary, as that would release essential

Growing, Preserving, and Using Herbs

oils before you can capture them in foods. Spread leaves in a single layer on a baking sheet. Preheat oven to 120°F, and place the baking sheet in the oven for five minutes. Remove and allow herbs to cool to room temperature. Store the leaves in airtight containers. Most cooks prefer to use glass or ceramic containers, as metal or plastic can affect the flavor of delicate herbs. Be sure to label the containers, not only with the name of the herb but also with the date. Store the containers in a cool, dark cupboard (not over the stove!) for up to a year.

To use home-dried herbs in recipes, crumble the leaves when measuring to get an accurate count, then proceed as directed.

Freezing Herbs for Fresh Flavor

Many chefs are discovering that frozen herbs have big flavor advantages. Herbs like chervil, chives, and cilantro, for example, are virtually tasteless when dried. Other herbs, like sage, become more harshly flavored. Moisture-filled herbs like basil and parsley are troublesome to dry without mechanical assistance.

If you freeze your herbs, on the other hand, you can capture fresh-picked flavor. Because the texture becomes mushy and the color darker, frozen herbs are best when you add them to cooked dishes like soups, stews, and sauces. Frozen herbs retain good flavor for 2 to 4 months.

You have a choice of several methods of freezing herbs:

Pack and freeze. For the least amount of fuss, simply pack herbs in freezer bags. If the stalks are tough, strip the leaves from the stems first. Label and date the bags and freeze.

Blanch and freeze. Some chefs find that blanching fresh herbs improves keeping power, especially with herbs like basil and lovage. Using tongs to hold the stem ends of the herbs, dip them in boiling water for 5 to 10 seconds, lift out, and sponge lightly between cotton towels to dry or whirl in a salad spinner. Place herbs in a self-sealing plastic freezer bag, then dip the bag in a bowl of cold water, being careful not to allow water into the opening. Press the bag to force out excess air, and seal. To use herbs frozen in this manner, break or slice off what you need and drop into soup or spaghetti sauce. Measure as for fresh herbs: two to three times the amount specified for dried herbs.

Puree and freeze. Another easy way to freeze herbs is to puree them in a blender, adding just enough water to make a slurry. Freeze the mixture in ice cube trays or plastic containers like recycled yogurt cups (note that pureed herbs will stain plastic ice cube trays). When the slurry is frozen, pop it out of the container and store in a labeled freezer bag. To use, drop a frozen cube into sauces, casseroles, or soup. If the additional water poses a problem with a recipe, thaw first, and strain out excess water.

Herb pastes. If you don't mind adding oil to a recipe, freezing herb pastes is an excellent way to retain fresh flavor. To make a paste, puree herbs, adding just enough vegetable oil to reduce herbs to a smooth paste — about ½ cup oil to 2 cups packed fresh herb leaves. It's easier to use a food processor to puree, but a blender will work if you stop the motor periodically and push the mixture down with a rubber spatula. Some cooks prefer to use extra-virgin olive oil to make herb pastes, especially if they plan to use the paste as a start to making pesto. If you're not sure how you'll be using the paste, however, use canola or sunflower oil, as either one adds less of its own flavor to the herb paste. Pack the herb paste in airtight, freezer-safe containers, such as yogurt containers. Label and date them. Freeze the paste immediately to avoid contamination.

Herb pastes are very convenient to use in any recipe calling for dried herbs, as the mixture doesn't freeze solid. Simply scoop out what you need with a spoon. Because the flavor is more concentrated, measure one-third to one-half less herb paste than the amount specified for dried herbs.

Safety first. *The combination of oil and fresh plant materials creates an environment that encourages the growth of bacteria. Use herb pastes immediately or keep them frozen.*

HERBAL *Resources*

SUPPLIERS OF FRESH AND DRIED HERBS

Diamond Organics
P.O. Box 2159
Freedom, CA 95019
Phone: 888-ORGANIC
Fax: 888-888-6777
e-mail: shop@diamondorganics.com
Web site: www.diamondorganics.com
Fresh organic herbs and edible flowers (fruits and vegetables, as well) airshipped overnight

AmeriHerb, Inc.
P.O. Box 1968
Ames, IA 50010
Phone: 800-267-6141
Fax: 515-232-8615
Dried herbs and spices in wholesale quantities

Mountain Rose Herbs
20818 High Street
North San Juan, CA 95960
Phone: 800-879-3337
Fax: 530-292-9138
Web site: www.botanical.com/mtrose/
Dried herbs, botanicals, and seasonings, as well as herb seeds, teas, and bodycare products

Penzey's Spices
P.O. Box 933
Muskego, WI 53150
Phone: 414-679-7207
Fax: 414-679-7207
e-mail: eblon@execpc.com
Web site: www.penzeys.com
Dried herbs, spices, and gourmet herb blends

SUPPLIERS OF HERB SEEDS AND PLANTS

Abundant Life Seed Foundation
P.O. Box 7722, 930 Lawrence Street
Port Townsend, WA 98368-0772
Phone: 360-385-5660
Fax: 360-385-7455
Nonprofit educational foundation committed to raising and collecting open-pollinated cultivars

Johnny's Selected Seeds
R.R. 1, Box 2580
Foss Hill Road
Albion, ME 04910-9731
Phone: 207-437-9294
Fax: 207-437-2165
e-mail: staff@johnnyseeds.com
Web site: www.johnnyseeds.com

George W. Park Seed Company
1 Parkton Avenue
Greenwood, SC 29647-0001
Phone: 800-845-3366
Fax: 800-209-0360
e-mail: info@parkseed.com
Web site: www.parkseed.com

Seed Savers Exchange
3094 North Winn Road
Decorah, IA 52101
Phone: 319-382-5990

The Thyme Garden
20546 Alsea Highway
Alsea, OR 97324
Phone: 541-487-8671
Fax: 541-487-8671
e-mail: thymegarden@proaxis.com
Web site: www.thymegarden.com

Well-Sweep Farm
205 Mount Bethel Road
Port Murray, NJ 07865
Phone: 908-852-5390
Fax: 908-852-1649

ORGANIC GARDENING SUPPLIES

Gardener's Supply Company
128 Intervale Road
Burlington, VT 05401
Phone: 800-863-1700
Fax: 802-863-3501
e-mail: info@gardeners.com
Web site: www.gardeners.com

Gardens Alive!
5100 Schenley Place
Lawrenceburg, IN 47025
Phone: 812-537-8698
Fax: 812-537-5108
e-mail: gardenhelp@gardens-alive.com
Web site: www.gardens-alive.com

The Natural Gardening Company
217 San Anselmo Avenue
San Anselmo, CA 94960
Phone: 707-766-9303
Fax: 707-766-9747
Web site: www.naturalgardening.com

BOTTLES, MINERALS, AND OTHER SUPPLIES

The Dasun Company
P.O. Box 668
Escondido, CA 92033
Phone: 800-433-8929
Zeolite

Frontier Natural Products Cooperative
P.O. Box 299
Norway, IA 52318
Phone: 800-669-3275
Fax: 800-717-4372
Web site: www.frontiercoop.com
Bulk non-irradiated herbs, essential oils, fixed oils, glycerin, lanolin, amber and clear glass bottles, strainers, incense charcoals, loofahs, scrub brushes, natural soaps, and many other supplies

Internet, Incorporated
7300 49th Avenue North
Minneapolis, MN 55428
Phone: 800-328-8456
Fax: 612-971-0872
e-mail: www.netting@internet.com
FDA-approved plastic netting suitable for drying racks

Lavender Lane
7337 #1 Roseville Road
Sacramento, CA 95842
Phone: 888-593-4400
Fax: 916-339-0842
e-mail: donna@lavenderlane.com
Web site: www.lavenderlane.com
Bottles, essential oils, diffusers, fixatives, fixed oils, fuller's earth, bentonite clay, lanolin, cocoa butter, beeswax, books; catalog: $2, refundable with order

Mid-Continent Agrimarketing, Inc.
1465 N. Winchester
Olathe, KS 66061-5881
Phone: 800-547-1392
Fax: 913-768-8968
Beeswax, paraffin, candle and soap molds, fixed oils, glycerin, glass bottles, metal and plastic bottle caps